To
Elizabeth Ann Ellingsen
My favorite middle child

Table Of Contents

Preface — 7

Ash Wednesday — 13
All Our Good Works And Generosity
Matthew 6:1-6, 16-21

Lent 1 — 19
The Temptations Of Christ And Our Temptations
Matthew 4:1-11

Lent 2 (C) — 27
Are You Born Again?
John 3:1-17 (C)

Lent 2 (RC) — 33
Where Have All The Visible Miracles Gone?
Matthew 17:1-9 (RC)

Lent 3 (C) — 39
Lent 2 (L)
Lent 3 (RC)
The Meeting Of Marriage Partners At The Well
John 4:5-26 (27-42) (C)
John 4:5-26 (27-30, 39-42) (L)
John 4:5-42 (RC)

Lent 4 (C, RC) — 47
Lent 3 (L)
We Must Be Blind!
John 9:1-41 (C, RC)
John 9:13-17, 34-49 (L)

Lent 4 (L) — 53
Competition In The Kingdom?
Matthew 20:17-28

Lent 5 — 59
The Resurrection Is Freedom!
John 11:(1-6) 17-45 (C)
John 11:1-53 (L)
John 11:1-45 (RC)

Sunday Of The Passion — 67
The Road To The Cross
Matthew 26:14—27:66 (C, RC)
Matthew 26:1—27:66 (L)

Palm Sunday — 75
God Works Through Opposites
Matthew 21:1-11 (C, L)

Maundy Thursday   81
   Wash Up First For The Meal Before You Eat!
   John 13:1-15 (C, RC)
   John 13:1-17, 34 (L)

Good Friday   89
   Why Did Jesus Have To Die?
   John 19:17-30

The Resurrection Of Our Lord   97
   The Empty Tomb
   John 20:1-18 (C, L)
   John 20:1-9 (RC)

Easter 2   103
   What Happens When We Can't Believe It?
   John 20:19-30

Easter 3   111
   What Happens To You When You Die?
   Luke 24:13-35

Easter 4   117
   Led By The Shepherd
   John 10:1-10

Easter 5   125
   Focus Your Faith
   John 14:1-14 (C)
   John 14:1-12 (L, RC)

Easter 6   131
   Good Works Will Not Save You!
   John 14:15-21

Easter 7   139
   The Majesty Of God's Love
   John 17:1-11

Ascension Day/Ascension Sunday (C, L)   145
   What Makes Those Disciples So Darn Happy?
   Luke 24:46-53 (C)
   Luke 24:44-53 (L)

Ascension Day/Ascension Sunday (RC)   149
   The Majesty Of God's Love
   Matthew 28:16-20 (RC)

Notes   157

C — Common Lectionary
L — Lutheran Lectionary
RC — Roman Catholic Lectionary

Preface

In Protestant churches, both among liturgical scholars and in the parishes, there is much disclarity about how the seasons of Lent and Easter should relate.[1] The great concern is that the center of the Christian faith, the Easter season, is receiving short shrift in the contemporary church. Until recently the liturgical calendar did not continue the Easter celebration of the resurrection for 50 days (as the liturgical calendar referred to Sundays after Easter). And in practice in most parishes the festival is still a one-day deal.

The problem with the celebration of Easter is in part related to the way in which the Protestant churches worship during the Easter season. The climate of joy and celebration which characterizes the Easter festival is not usually apparent in the worship services of most congregations in the Sundays following Easter. They are not celebrations of the resurrection. Likewise, the sermons for these Sundays do not always proclaim the presence of the Risen Lord and the new life he has given. The sermons in the second half of this volume aim to compensate for the latter deficiency — to proclaim the manifestation of Christ, his presence among us and the new life which is ours. If combined with a celebrative mood in worship, the ideas and themes of these sermons (if God makes his Word out of the reader's adaptation) may help extend the Easter celebration a few weeks (hopefully seven weeks) after the beginning of the festival. The reader will note that as this series of sermons gets closer to the Festival of the Ascension, the glorification of Christ, a Trinitarian framework for reflections on the nature of Christian living becomes more explicit. This theological emphasis was quite self-conscious on my part, for I am convinced that a key to spiritual and ecumenical renewal in the Western churches would be to help the faithful appreciate what a profound resource the Trinity doctrine can be for their spiritual lives.

The centrality of the Easter festival may be clouded in ways not just related to how we celebrate the Easter season. Its centrality may also be compromised by the way in which the church commemorates Lent. Even in Protestant churches, official attitudes toward Lent are still permeated by the medieval manner of observing the season. Recall that the medieval observance of the season involved a spirit of penitence, including rigorous spiritual discipline (such as fasting) in order to appease God. The evangelical aim of such practices was to prepare the faithful for Easter by helping to intensify an awareness of sin so that the meaning and significance of Christ's passion and resurrection would be all the more existentially significant. In the post-Reformation church this medieval atmosphere was retained, and Lent became (for some Protestants still is) a season for concentrating exclusively on the history of Christ's passion. In this way, so the liturgical logic goes, we are brought to penitence by being reminded of the depth of our sin in seeing what we have done to Christ.

At least since mid-century, liturgical scholars have objected to these emphases. The concern has been that a commemoration of Lent with this focus on the passion fails to prepare the faithful for Easter. Indeed such emphases prepare the faithful for the events of Holy Week. But with a focus on the persecution and the sufferings of Christ, Lent has been reduced merely to a preparation for Good Friday, not for the proclamation of the new life given at Easter. The result of such liturgical praxis has been an inadvertent de-emphasis of Christianity's high holy day. Are such practices one of the reasons why Christian worship and congregational life are serious and somber business in so many congregations?

How can we recycle the centrality of Easter in our celebration of the entire Easter cycle (both the Easter and Lenten seasons)? The title of this book indicates that I want to affirm the preparatory character of Lent. I would even go further in endorsing aspects of the medieval commemoration of the season by maintaining its penitential themes. Lent is indeed properly a time for us to re-experience the depth of our sin and to repent of it, so that we may be better prepared for the miracle of divine forgiveness which Easter brings. But if we confess that this new life is the work of God and that our salvation is solely by grace (Ephesians 2:8), then the preparation of Lent must itself be God's work and linked to the new life. How can that Word be proclaimed?

We may discern some clues for answering the question of what to make of Lent as a season of preparation in an evangelical context, by recalling the origins of the season in the early church. Recall that in that period of church history baptism was generally celebrated on Easter. Since most baptisms were baptisms of believers, the early church used a period prior to Easter to catechize (instruct) the candidates for baptism. Thus Lent does not just have penitential origins. It was also a season for instruction in the faith, in preparation for baptism. In its 21st century, if not now already in the '90s, could the church link together both the medieval (penitential/preparatory) roots of Lent and its patristic (instructional/baptismal) themes by more strongly emphasizing the links between preparation and repentance on one side, and baptism and the new life, on the other?

The sermons for the Lenten season contained in this volume endeavor to make these connections between preparation through penitence and the new life given in baptism. The gospel lessons assigned for the season provide excellent occasions to practice such liturgical proclamation. In the stories about Jesus' ministry leading up to and through Holy Week we discover ourselves in the characters who surround him. Their feebleness and lack of faith are our sin. And such sinfulness stands out all the more sharply in relation to Christ, who is the first fruits of the new life given at Easter (1 Corinthians 15:23; Colossians 1:18). Thus the new life in Christ and penitence for sin as a preparation for the new life are held together in such cases. Penitence and preparation happen in the presence of Christ and the new life he gives. Thus they are God's work.

On other occasions our texts concentrate only on Jesus and his reactions to various trials and temptations. Again we may discover ourselves in such accounts. Our baptisms have united us with Christ, so that his suffering is ours (done on our behalf) and his conquest of sin is our liberation from it (Romans 6:1-11). In these cases too, it is evident that our penitence and preparation are really God's work, given in our baptism. And these realities are inextricably linked to the new life which the Easter event makes manifest. The connection of all these themes through our baptism, the central role played by this sacrament as the theological framework for the Lenten season, is further undergirded by explicit references to baptism in several of the assigned texts.[2]

In order to help hearers identify with the characters of these gospel texts, most of the sermons have employed the biblical narrative approach which I have advocated in earlier books.[3] Of course I have not employed this in developing every sermon in the book. On a few occasions, a more didactic approach seemed more appropriate. After all, variety is the spice of good pulpit life.

In any case, the basic supposition of the biblical narrative approach is that we should read the Bible, not as a source book for the history of the early church, but as a piece of great literature. Thus the tools of literary analysis provide the most appropriate approach for interpreting and preaching on its texts. This entails that one reads and presents the Epistles as letters, the gospels and Old Testament histories as realistic narratives, et cetera. This analytical approach necessarily entails that we identify ourselves and our hearers with the characters in these texts. For no one reads a letter without pretending that they are the recipient. And good realistic narratives or novels inevitably draw us into the stories so that we feel that we are a part of them.

It is perhaps appropriate to add some existential reflections to these theological ruminations on the background of the sermons in this volume. The themes of despair over sin (preparation) and rejoicing over new life (manifestation) are most appropriate topics for this book of sermons. They were written and delivered in a period of some despair about the direction of my ministry followed immediately by another period of rejoicing about a new direction.

I hope that some of my existential feelings have been conveyed by the words of these sermon texts. Yet, nonetheless, I would urge readers and users of these sermons to put their own feelings and faith into the sermons, to enter into a dialogue with them. Especially remember this plea if they are used from the pulpit. In their present form the sermons have been written for the eye, not for the ear. The preacher who used them would need to rewrite the texts "for the ear" by breaking up the longer phrases with repetitions, by inserting pauses at appropriate points, and by the use of contractions wherever it is natural.

Throughout my up-and-down periods of writing, as always, I have been accompanied by my regular partners in (theological and familial) crime. Were there space I would also mention all my many friends and supporters in the theological community, from whom I have learned so much (among whom I include the professional staff of C.S.S.), and all the members of my dear extended family. But as usual, express thanks are most deserved by the people with whom I reside. My wife Betsey, with all the work she did in editing and typing the manuscript, not to mention her friendship, would seem to deserve the most thanks. But then she is receiving such official commendation in the dedication of another soon-to-be published book.

It may seem an act of unwise favoritism for a father of three to dedicate a book to only one of his children, especially when the honored one is part of a set of twins. Worse yet may seem such a dedication when it is known that all three of these children aid in the writing and preparation process by bringing joy to the author through their animated presences. Of course, the eldest already has received credit, as a 1990 book of mine, written before the birth of children two and three, was dedicated only to him. And now I have another book, the prospect for which can bear the name of the youngest when it comes out. Consequently, it only seems just that my favorite middle child, Elizabeth Ann, would get this one — a book for every young Ellingsen. Someday, when she learns how to talk, she and my youngest may rival their older brother in making creative contributions to my writing by the precocious questions they ask. With helpers like that, an author and preacher can't go wrong.

Ash Wednesday
Matthew 6:1-6, 16-21

All Our Good Works And Generosity

Jesus was giving his famous Sermon on the Mount. In the middle of it he looked at the disciples from his sitting position (as was customary for Jewish rabbis of the first century when they were teaching). And Jesus said: "Beware of practicing your piety before men in order to be seen by them; for then you will have no reward from your Father who is in heaven (Matthew 6:1)."

To whom was Jesus referring with these words? He was probably talking here and at other points in the sermon about the Pharisees. Recall that the Pharisees were the most devout Jews, the most religious people, of Jesus' day. Jesus was talking about people like us.[1]

People like us? Our commitment to our Lord and his work is obvious, is it not? Here it is a Wednesday, and we have come to his house for worship. For the next weeks most of us are committed to worshiping him at least twice a week. Why, think of it. Some of us may return even a third time weekly for some other congregational activity. I clearly speak to a committed group of believers.

In all seriousness, those of us gathered for this worship experience do take our faith seriously. More than likely among your circle of acquaintances, you do not mind if they know that you are a Christian, and even a church-goer. Do you even take some pleasure in being known in this way? How much pleasure do you take? Is it not nice to be known around town or in your circle as a decent human being, an upstanding, solid citizen, even a leader in your church? Do you not enjoy having that kind of reputation? Is it ever an incentive to work for this parish? In that case, Jesus' words condemn you and the rest of us: "Beware of practicing your piety before men in order to be seen by them; for then you will have no reward from your Father who is in heaven (Matthew 6:1)."

Jesus next proceeded to condemn us further: "Thus when you give alms, sound no trumpet before you, as the hypocrites do in the synagogues and in the streets, that they may be praised by men. Truly I say to you, they have their reward. But when you give alms do not let your left hand know what your right hand is doing, so that your alms may be in secret . . . (Matthew 6:2-4)."

It really is incredible among the very best of people how few of us there truly are who seek to do good without also seeking honor or worldly credit. I want a pat on the back for the good I do, don't you?

That ugly side of our personalities comes out the clearest when saints like us get angry or feel a bit miffed when the recipients of our benevolence are ungrateful. If our motivation had not been to receive the world's thanks, we would not become so disgusted with ingratitude, would we? Have you not ever felt such feelings? I have, and our Lord's words condemn me.

Have you ever come shuffling away from an ingrate saying, "I have done so much for her, and she has forgotten it already. People are so ungrateful!" Or perhaps you have made the point this way: "I would be happy to take the soul out of my body and give it to him. But since I see that this kindness would be wasted on him, because he is such an undeserving fellow and does not even come from a good family, he can go to hell before he'll get a crust of bread from me." By such thoughts, so common to us all, we betray our real motivation for doing good, namely, to have people praise and worship us instead of God. Oh what a shameful distortion of good works are you and I now engaged in!

Jesus still talks about giving alms in secret, so that the left hand does not know what the right hand is doing. There is much debate among biblical scholars about what he meant at this point, but I rather like Martin Luther's version of it. Luther claimed that Jesus urged the faithful not to inform the left hand what the right hand is doing when alms are given, because otherwise the left hand will try to take more away than the right hand gave.[2]

Is that not our way of dealing with people? If we offer some gift or act of kindness to a person, we imagine that we have bought her and that she is so deeply obligated to us that she dare not say a word except what we want to hear. Of course most people do not notice our expectations and we even manage to deceive ourselves concerning our real intentions. But in fact our faith commitments and good works are nothing but a vain pretense.

Can we do no good works? How about prayer? And Jesus said: "And when you pray you must not be like the hypocrites; for they love to stand and pray in the synagogues and at the street corners, that they may be seen by men. Truly, I say to you, they have their reward. But when you pray, go into your room and shut the door and pray to your Father who is in secret . . . (Matthew 6:5-6)"

Even our prayer is tainted by our quest for worldly reward or merit. How often are we inclined to tell our dear ones or acquaintances that we have prayed for them in a time of need. What really is our motive for reporting this to the one for whom we say we have prayed? Is our need to report on our prayer life to others related just a bit to a desire to make an impression on people and because we enjoy having a reputation for deep faith and piety? Pastors are especially vulnerable to this disease, because we want our people to believe that we care about them and that we walk with God. I have been associated with a Southern parish where certain lay people have reported on the prayers they claimed to offer on behalf of those with whom they were arguing for the sole purpose of winning sympathy for their own side of the dispute. I have seen what the leaders of that "religious" haven have done to those for whom they reportedly prayed. Such prayers belong in the dung heap; they are not worth a pile of ashes. We are all guilty of praying with this kind of motivation sometimes.

A pile of ashes. All our works, even our good works, amount to nothing, because they are marred by sin. Even our faith, our commitment to the work of the church, the good works we do on behalf of others, and our prayers are infected by the tint of selfishness and evil. This is Jesus' point also at the end of our gospel lesson (also see Romans 7:18). He proceeds to warn us not to lay up treasures on earth for ourselves, because moth and rust consume and thieves break in and steal. Far better, he says, we should lay up for ourselves treasures in heaven which will not be destroyed by moth, rust and thievery. Where your treasures are, that is where your heart is.

Some have understood Jesus to be condemning gluttony or undue preoccupation with material goods at this point. Yet much more is he teaching a lesson here about the first commandment, and our failure to keep it. To say that our treasures determine our heart, as Jesus says, is just another way of claiming that our treasures determine our ultimate loyalties, our god. Jesus makes it clear that this is his point at the end of the chapter from which we have been reading, when he tells his disciples and us first to seek God's kingdom, and then all worldly things will be ours.

Order your priorities, the first commandment teaches. But inevitably we fail to get it right. This is why all our works, even the very best ones like faith, commitment to the work of the church, kindnesses shown to others, even our prayers, are marred. They are ultimately or at least polluted by expressions of our lust for influence, reputation and pride. They do not add up to a pile of ashes after all.

A pile of ashes. That is what Ash Wednesday is all about. A reminder that all we do and are, apart from the new life given in Christ, is nothing but a pile of ashes.

Of course Ash Wednesday, the first day of Lent, owes its name to the medieval practice of imposing ashes on the faithful. (We are doing it today.) The whole point of this practice is apparent in what is said to the faithful as the ashes are imposed on them. The priest or the pastor quotes God's Word to Adam and Eve when he banished them from Eden on account of their sin (Genesis 3:19). "You are dust, and unto dust you will return." You are dust, and to dust you will return.

The ashes of Ash Wednesday remind us that all we are and do must end in death. So it is that even our "good" deeds, because they are marred by selfishness and sin, ultimately lead us to death. Such good works are nothing more than another nail in our coffin.

No room is left here for spiritual pride. The very best of our deeds deserve the judgment of hell. They are some of the reasons that we must die. The words of today's psalm hit the nail on the head: "For I know my transgressions, and my sin is ever before me. Against thee, thee only, have I sinned, and done that which is evil in thy sight, so that thou are justified in thy sentence and blameless in thy judgment . . . (Psalm 51:3-4)."

In the midst of such an awareness of our sin, the only possible reaction is repentance. Again the words of our psalm are our song: "Have mercy on me, O God, according to thy steadfast love, according to thy abundant mercy blot out my transgressions. Wash me thoroughly from my iniquity, and cleanse me from my sin! (Psalm 51:1-2)."

Coming to know the depth of our sin. Driving us to repentance. That is what Ash Wednesday is all about. But that is not the final word! Repentance is not an end in itself. It has another end in view — preparation for new life (in Christ).

Again our psalm as well as our gospel says it all: "Fill me with joy and gladness; let the bones which thou hast broken rejoice. Hide thy face from my sins, and blot out all my iniquities. Create in me a clean heart, O God, and put a new and right spirit within me (Psalm 51:8-10)."

What is this new heart and right spirit that we faithfully await? Our gospel lesson gave us some hints. It is evident in the life that Jesus lived. That is what the new life is like.

The gospel lesson also describes the new life as a life totally dedicated to God and to serving him. A life whose deeds care nothing about human acclaim or reputation. A life of total freedom, freedom from anxieties about what people think of us. Total freedom, because good works just come spontaneously, not as a result of constraint or scheming for power, position and a good reputation. (John 8:36; Ephesians 2:8-10, Psalms 110:3).

The freedom of this new life, which is given at Easter and the joy that comes with it mean just a little more when we are adequately prepared for it by an awareness of how much we need it. By an awareness of how hopelessly trapped we are by our sin; by an awareness that the good works we do on our own are nothing but a pile of ashes. Thank God for the ashes and the meaning behind them. Keep in mind how thoroughly mired in sin you are the next time you feel good about one of your apparent good deeds. But also be sure you thank God, too. Thank God for the new life he gives you!

Lent 1
Matthew 4:1-11

The Temptations Of Christ And Our Temptations

Then Jesus was led up by the Spirit into the wilderness to be tempted by the devil . . . And the tempter came and said to him, "If you are the Son of God, command these stones to becomes loaves of bread (Matthew 4:1-3)."

Some of the worst temptations seem to come when you are alone, do they not? Of course we are tempted by individuals and sometimes by the crowd. But even in those instances the struggle that their temptations occasion happen in us. Consequently even on those occasions we face the temptation alone, just like Jesus did.

Matthew's narrative also refers to the devil's role in tempting Jesus. Regardless of what you think of a personal devil, all of us can agree that we have experienced something like what Jesus experienced. Even when we are alone when we are tempted, it is as if someone else, something bigger than we, does the tempting. I think of temptation along the lines that Paul described in Romans 7:15: "For I do not do what I want [he says], but I do the very thing I hate." Then again in verse 23 of that chapter he writes: ". . . but I see in my members another law at war with the law of my mind and making me captive to the law of sin which dwells in my members." Temptation, sin and evil. They are bigger than we are. And so

Jesus encountered temptations bigger than he was, in the form of the devil.

How revealing it is that Jesus endured temptations at the start of his ministry. Is that not when temptations often come to us — when we are just beginning or contemplating the beginning of new phases in our lives? How often temptations then encounter us in the depth of our being?

Jesus faced three temptations that time in the wilderness. What was the first temptation? To command the stones to become loaves of bread. It is hardly a temptation that we face. Or is it?

Are not those of us with high ideals, the reformers among us, tempted by this one? In Jesus' case, the temptation was that he should devote the bulk of his ministry to social and economic reform, not to spiritual matters. Is there not a temptation for thoughtful, caring Christians like us in the waning stages of the 20th century, caught up by our social consciousness and blitzed by the media with an awareness of the poverty and oppression all around us, to think that economic and social reform is more important than other people's or our own spiritual well-being? That is a difficult temptation for me sometimes.

When Jesus was tempted to turn the stones to bread, to focus his ministry on social and economic reform, the character of his Messiahship and his service to God was being tempted to manifest his Messiahship primarily as a miracle worker. You see, in Jesus' day many Jews had come to believe that, in the day of salvation, the miracles of Israel's journey through the wilderness during the Exodus under Moses would be repeated. Thus like Moses, the Messiah would be expected to provide manna from heaven (Exodus 16:15-36).[1] And just as the miracles that God did through Moses helped set the people of Israel free, so the Jews of Jesus' day expected the Messiah to perform similar miracles that would set the Jews of the day free from the social injustice of Roman tyranny.

Are not we tempted in a similar vein? Like the Jews of Jesus' day, we want God to make his presence known to us through miracles — visible miracles. We are not content with the ones we already have (like the preaching of the Word, the administering of the sacraments, and all the material blessings he has showered upon us). How much we idealists yearn for a more visible demonstration by God of his will by his overcoming the poverty and oppression that still lives on in the world. If God would only do that, we say, then we could truly believe in him.

Jesus finally said "no" to this temptation. He said "no" to it, by invoking the correct priorities in God's plan for redeeming the world. God places a priority on his Word over visible, verifiable miracles and even over social justice. Jesus cites God's Word in scripture to ward off the temptation. The words of Deuteronomy 8:3 rolled from his mouth: "Man shall not live by bread alone, but by every word that proceeds from the mouth of God."

The Word of God was our Lord's sure defense against that (first) temptation. Likewise it is the proclamation of the Word and spiritual growth which we are called to prioritize over a concern for visible miracles in the realm of social justice and the alleviation of poverty.

Next Jesus experienced a second temptation. It was not unlike the first one. The tempter urges Jesus to proceed to Jerusalem, to climb to the top of the temple, and then to jump. Then when God saved Jesus, everybody would be convinced that Jesus was the Messiah. This is the temptation to sensationalism. The temptation to shock, to offend, in order to accomplish the good, or, worse yet, in order to attract attention. This is the temptation to test God by doing things contrary to his usual means of dealing with us. I refer here to the temptation to do irresponsible things and then say to ourselves: "Well, if there's really a God, he would protect us. Put it in God's hands (no matter how irresponsible we are). If there really is a God, he'll save us."

An attitude like this, a desire for visible miracles to establish or confirm our faith, represents a deep spiritual discontent with God's visible means of ministering to his people.

Such discontent is nothing more than a manifestation of our works-righteousness — a desire to create a right relationship with God on our own terms. It is nothing but works-righteousness.[2]

We all know about this temptation, do we not? If not, you surely know about the temptation to sensationalism — the desire to have people notice you no matter what it takes. Yes, we all have firsthand experience of Jesus' temptations. Again he appeals to God's Word in response; this time, specifically to Deuteronomy 6:16: "You shall not tempt the Lord your God."

This brings us to the third temptation that Jesus endured. It is also not unrelated to the first temptation, except this time it is on a larger, more tempting note. Jesus is tempted by the messenger of falsehood to do what everybody in Israel expected the Messiah to do — to be a political leader who would conquer the kingdoms that oppressed the Jews. Does not the world also tempt us with the promise of power? Do we not yearn to achieve — to be famous, to exercise influence, to be somebody in the community or in the company whom everybody admires or perhaps regards with a bit of fear?

Oh, but Jesus saw through the tempter's ruse. His tempter wanted him to worship evil. That is what sin really is, according to Martin Luther. In writing about the first commandment ("You shall have no other gods"), Luther wrote that "a god is that to which we look for all good and in which we find refuge in every time of need . . . As I have often said, the trust and faith of the heart alone make both God and an idol."[3] In short, what you make most important of all in your life is really your god.

The story of this third temptation here in Matthew's gospel makes this point. Had Jesus or we fallen for this or been lured away by the temptation to achieve worldly power, then worldly power and influence would be our god — and not the God of Abraham, Isaac and Jacob. Too often we are idolators, are we not? Too often we are tempted to make worldly power and influence the god of our lives, the most important thing for which we live. We know how Jesus was tempted; it is our temptation, too.

Jesus' response to this temptation is again instructive. Once again he appeals to the Word of God and quotes the Old Testament Scripture. This time he appeals to Deuteronomy 6:13: "You shall worship the Lord your God and him only shall you serve."

This third appeal to the Word of God by Jesus was the turning point. The devil, three times defeated, left him. Then angels came and ministered to Jesus. He had conquered. Never again would God's victory over evil be in doubt.[4]

What does it all mean for us? Of course, the story has meaning for us insofar as it has helped us to consider and become more aware of the temptations we face. We might have overlooked them, more easily fallen prey to them, had we not been reminded of our desire to have God redeem the world in accord with our private wishes, of our discontent with his visible means, of our works-righteousness, and of our desire for power and influence. Seeing Jesus grapple with those temptations reminds us that his struggles are ours. And in being called to an awareness of these temptations, we come to an awareness of our need for the new life that Christ gives. We have been better prepared for the blessing of Easter.

Of course, there is also a real comfort in the realization that Jesus has struggled with the same temptations we face. It makes God and Jesus a little more real, a little more in touch with us and our weaknesses. It makes it easier to relate to our God as a friend, because he has been there with us. Yet the nagging question remains: How can these temptations that Jesus has shared with us be overcome? Granted, he has conquered them. But he is God. How does this conquest of the temptations that we face help us to overcome them?

Jesus' invocation of God's Word to ward off the tempter provides some hints. Yet, somehow that awareness in itself is not too comforting. For it makes me feel like I have to do something if I have to fight temptation the way Jesus did. It seems as if I must cling to the Word. And, of course, my faith is not as strong as his; I may not have the perseverance and faith that he had. Indeed I surely do not.

Thank God, however, that there is a word of gospel in the midst of Jesus' conquest of his temptations. As I suggested earlier, his conquest of temptation points to Jesus' final victory over sin and evil on Easter. And that is a victory in which you and I share!

How can we obtain the blessings of Christ's victory, the assurance that in him we can successfully struggle with our temptations? Jesus' own means of overcoming the temptations that he faced offer us some clues. He appealed to the Word of God. And it is through the Word that we share in his victory.

Recall that the Word comes to us in several forms. It comes to us not just in scripture, the form that Jesus employed in overcoming temptation. The Word of God also comes in visible form through sacraments like baptism. In fact, in baptism we already share in Jesus' conquest. For in your baptism you received all that belongs to Christ.

This theme is too often overlooked, I am afraid. Our failure to recognize it and to live by this insight accounts for why so often Christian life is regarded as a burden, why fighting temptation is regarded as something we have to do. Yet the idea that in baptism we have received all that Christ has is solidly rooted in scripture. Listen to what Paul says about it in the sixth chapter of Romans (v. 4). He says: "We were buried therefore with him by baptism into death, so that as Christ was raised from the dead by the glory of the Father, we too might walk in newness of life."

In your baptism you received Christ, so that the new life in him that conquered death and evil on Easter is yours. The great 16th century reformer John Calvin put it this way: "Lastly, our faith receives from baptism the advantage of its sure testimony to us that we are not only engrafted into the death and life of Christ, but so united to Christ himself that we become sharers in all his blessings."[5]

Sharers in all his blessings. And in one of his sermons, Martin Luther put these words in Christ's mouth: "If you are baptized and believe in me, then you are the man who has more and can perform greater things, yes, can do the same works that I am now doing, and even greater works than these."[6]

We can do the same works as our Lord. In your baptism you have been given all that Christ is and has done. His victory over temptation is yours! Jesus himself put it this way once to his followers: "Behold, I have given you authority to tread upon serpents and scorpions, and over all the power of the enemy; and nothing shall hurt you (Luke 10:19)."

Nothing shall hurt you. We have the authority to overcome the enemy, to overcome all temptations. In our baptisms everything that Christ has becomes yours and mine. His conquest of the temptations that we face is ours.

Keep that in mind the next time you are tempted. Remember that Christ has shared those same temptations that you are now facing. Then lean on him. And remember that he already has defeated those temptations for you. His victory is ours! It is not we who must fight the temptations that we experience. God, side-by-side with us, fights them for us!

Lent 2
John 3:1-17 (C)

Are You Born Again?

It was late, almost bedtime, when the Jewish leader came to Jesus' residence. Into Jesus' presence came Nicodemus, one of the best-known Jewish professors in all of Israel (a member of the Jewish Sanhedrin). Nicodemus finally reached the short ruddy-faced leader of the disciples, and he said to him, "Rabbi, we know that you are a teacher come from God; for no one can do these signs that you do unless God is with him (John 3:2)."

However, Jesus then said something very strange. It really amounted to a put-down of Nicodemus. It was a strange move on Jesus' part, because here he was, a common, ordinary, lower middle class preacher, being honored by a visit from the respected and well-known Nicodemus. On top of that, the eminent Nicodemus was even acknowledging that Jesus actually had something important to say. Now he was present, wanting to know more. The great master willing to sit at the lowly Jesus' feet!

What Jesus actually did was to tell Nicodemus that he did not really understand anything at all. "Truly, truly, I say to you, unless one is born anew, he cannot see the kingdom of God (John 3:3)." In short, Jesus was really saying: "Nicodemus, unless you have been born again, you do not have the foggiest idea what I am saying. You don't know anything!" Quite a put-down. "Have you been born again, Nicodemus?"

It was an early spring/late winter Sunday afternoon, kind of like today. You had been to church in the morning and now were out for a stroll with the family. (Perhaps it happened on a Monday like tomorrow at the office.) On the other side of the park (or the office) you could see your neighbor/colleague Nora making her way in your direction. "Hi, friend," Nora called out. "Oh no," you say to yourself. "I hope she isn't going to start talking to me about that church she attends. Every time we talk, it seems to be the same story."

Sure enough this encounter was not different. "You just would not have believed how meaningful our service was," Nora began. On and on she went, talking about the hymns, the healings, the speaking in tongues, and the altar calls that had happened that day. As she went on you tried to be polite and listened, but your boredom with the whole thing was obvious. Even Nora finally realized it.

"I guess this whole thing doesn't interest you much, does it?" Nora asked. "Well, I wouldn't say that," you fumbled back. "Oh, yes," Nora replied. "You're bored. I guess I should have realized it all along. The people who go to your congregation, they may go to church most every week just like you do, but you don't really know the Lord Jesus Christ. He is not really in your heart. You haven't been born again. And until you have been born again, you have nothing."

Have you been born again? Have you been born again? How many times have you been asked that question or at least heard about it being asked? What does it mean to be born again?

In the minds of most people, perhaps for most of us, being born again seems to have to do with a conversion to Christianity where the power of God becomes especially real. It has to do with that one moment in life where we break with the past and come to Christ. People who talk this way about being born again can usually tell you the exact day and how it happened. Consequently, someone like Billy Graham can tell you how he was born again in a meeting led by Mordecai Ham in 1934, and how he has never been the same.

All this talk about being born again seems calculated to make members of mainline denominational traditions feel guilty. At least I know it always made me feel guilty. The problem is that most of us have grown up in the church and lived with it our whole lives. Oh sure, some of us may have spent a few years away from the church. Yet just the same, we cannot seem to put our finger on any exact time when Christ came into our life.

Worse yet, even if we could pick out an exact time when we came to Christ, it does not seem like there is anything much different about our lives. To be sure we try to live like Christians. Yet we continue making mistakes: We are unkind and inconsiderate; we lose our temper; we gossip; we may even cheat and steal. And so we wonder and worry about just how good a Christian we are. The result is that texts like today's gospel lesson which talk about being born again make us feel awfully guilty.

Oh, but they need not. Such texts need not impose guilt, because when the Bible talks about being born again it means something quite different from what many Christians and the secular media think it is. In fact being born again has nothing to do with something we do. In addition, being born again certainly does not mean that you will never think or do anything wrong again. People who think this way simply have not read their Bibles closely enough.

For instance, consider again our gospel lesson for today. To be sure, it talks about being born again. But then it elaborates the theme a bit more. Yes, Jesus tells Nicodemus that he must be born again. Yet then Jesus gives him and us the answer — the answer to the question of what it means to be born again. "Truly, truly, I say to you, unless one is born of water and the Spirit, he cannot enter the kingdom of God (John 3:5)." Unless you are baptized, born of water and Spirit. That is what it means to be born again: To be baptized and to receive God's love.

This emphasis on baptism as a born-again event is consistent with the teaching of scripture (see Titus 3:5).[1] This often overlooked viewpoint makes it a whole new ball game with respect to what is important in the Christian faith. Since baptism comes at the beginning of life for most of us, then that means that we are born again at the very beginning of our Christian lives. Consequently being born again does not depend on our having any special feelings, special visions, or anything like that. To be born again, according to the Bible and the teachings of our church, is simply to focus on what God has done for us, not what we have done for God.

At first this line of thinking may sound a bit confusing, but not if you reflect on it for a time. For the church is committed to emphasizing God and his work, not what we do for him. Our salvation does not depend on the way we lead our lives; it does not depend on our having warm, glowing feelings about God which assure me that I am born again; salvation does not depend on us at all. Our salvation depends only on Jesus Christ, and that has long ago been accomplished (Romans 3:21ff; Galatians 2:16). Consequently, even in the times when my Christian life does not measure up, I still have the promise of God's love.

One of the crucial themes of the Lenten season, one of the disciplines of preparation for hearing the gospel of God's love, is that we not take ourselves too seriously. For the first step in hearing the Easter message properly is an awareness that, on the basis of the lives we lead or the depth of our spirituality, we do not have a chance for salvation. It all depends on God.

Martin Luther summarized the nature of Christian life, what it is like to be born again, very well in one of his lectures in 1535. He reported that his teacher, John von Staupitz, said to him: " 'It pleases me very much that this doctrine of ours gives glory and everything else solely to God and nothing at all to men; for it is as clear as day that it is impossible to ascribe too much glory, goodness, etc., to God.' . . . And it is true that the doctrine of the gospel takes away all glory, wisdom, righteousness, etc., from men and gives it solely to the Creator, who makes all things out of nothing. Furthermore, it is far safer to ascribe too much to God than to man."[2]

"Christ must increase and we must decrease." The liturgy of the Roman Catholic mass conveys this theme very well. On receiving the sacrament, the congregation responds: "Lord, I am not worthy . . ."

The message of today's gospel lesson is that we may best prepare ourselves for the new life of the Easter gospel by not placing too much emphasis on ourselves. Merely because we are active in the church or have lived good lives does not entail that we have earned God's love. Far from it. Nor should we imagine that a good tingly feeling about God or a sudden conversion is our ticket into heaven. We ought not to think this way, for salvation hinges on God.

There is a positive side to this denial of any human contribution to our salvation, to such a de-emphasizing of the emotional, experiential side of being born again. It may be that your Christian faith and lifestyle are deficient and you do not feel born again. That is the state of my all-too-deficient spiritual life. Yet it does not matter. Can you recite the creed? Do you believe it? Then you have faith, and you can be assured that God loves you. That is what Jesus says about himself in our gospel lesson: "Whoever believes in him [in me] may have eternal life (John 3:15).''

God has always loved you. We really are all born-again Christians here this morning. We became born again the day we were baptized. We became born again on the cross at Calvary in 32 A.D., for on that day God proclaimed to the world that he loved us. Now nothing can separate us from that love (see Romans 8:38-39).

Have you been baptized? Then, my friends, you have been born again! You are brand new. All your short-comings, feelings of guilt — that is not the real you. Your baptism prepares you to struggle with them, prepares you to hear and believe the gospel. For the real you is loved by God already, and that is both a preparation for our struggles against insecurity and evil as well as an accomplished fact. In baptism, you have been born again!

Lent 2 (RC)
Matthew 17:1-9

Where Have All The Visible Miracles Gone?

Today we celebrate the miracle of transfiguration. It is a great story — a great way to continue our Lenten discipline of preparing for the Easter season. Jesus takes three of his disciples up on a mountain with him, and before their very eyes he is swallowed up by the glory of God's great might. In the presence of such glory, his clothes turn white as light and his face shines like the sun. Then Moses and Elijah, two men of God who had been dead for more than 1,000 and more than 800 years respectively, appeared before Jesus and his disciples, and they started talking with him. By now the disciples were really uneasy, scared. They had never seen anything like this. Then to top it off a voice from heaven could be heard: "This is my beloved Son, with whom I am well pleased; listen to him (Matthew 17:5)."

Yes, it is a great story. Yet we have here a text that presents itself as a most difficult pericope on which to prepare a sermon/homily. To be sure, the miracle of the transfiguration reveals to us God's great power. Who else could do these great and mighty things but God? Indeed the power and glory of God are greater than we can even imagine. What great miracles he is able to do!

On the other hand, the fact that God can do such great miracles like the transfiguration can be a little embarrassing for modern Catholics. For with the exception of a few Vatican-documented miracles by modern saints, God does not seem to be performing such natural miracles today, at least not in our parish or in our diocese. Some Protestants and our own charismatics who have healing services claim to behold such miracles. Consequently the miracle of the transfiguration raises for us a very serious question: Why are great natural miracles like that not happening in our parish? Why do we not have regular healing services? After all, Jesus did it, so why should not we, his followers? Why are we not speaking in tongues this morning? What has happened to our faith in the great glory and miraculous power of God?

Questions like these are being posed to us Roman Catholics as well as to many mainline Protestant denominations by the charismatic movement. Basically charismatics say that the rest of us Christians have been so modernized and sophisticated that we are a bit embarrassed by the Bible and the tradition. It is time to return to these sources of our faith!

If you are serious about a revival of passion for the sources of our faith, then you cannot help but notice that, in scripture as well as in the subsequent tradition of the church, God was always doing great natural, visible miracles. Christians inspired by the Holy Spirit spoke "in tongues." God revealed his majesty and spoke from heaven, like in the transfiguration. Those things happened in the past; they were performed by God; why not now? And if you say that miracles do not happen today, that God does not often do them anymore, are you not denying God? These are the questions posed to us and our Protestant friends by the charismatics.

Perhaps you have never been exposed to charismatics and had these questions directly addressed to you. Yet have you ever wondered why great natural miracles like the transfiguration are not more often happening today among Catholics? Have you ever wondered why more parishes in our diocese do not have healing services today the way that Jesus and the disciples used to do it? Ever wondered?

I used to raise these questions. Ever since childhood I used to wonder why God did not perform a host of natural miracles like he once did. I asked and asked until one day I got the courage to ask one of the great unsung Christian theologians of our day — a Scandinavian layman by the name of Emil Ellingsen. [Note: Priest may substitute his own father's name and nationality.] "Dad," I said. (I always called him "Dad.") "Dad, how come God does not do any miracles anymore?" The great theologian took his time with the question, looked at me very intently — as is his custom. He looked at me, and then in his slight Brooklyn accent, he said, "Because God knows we don't need 'em so much anymore, Mark."

We do not need them anymore. That answer has stayed with me, and I have especially kept it in mind during the last few years, not so much because it was an answer given to a seven-year-old child by a father whom the child very much did and still respects. That is a good reason to remember my father's answer, but it is not a sufficient justification for using it in a sermon/homily. There is a better reason for sharing my father's response with you. It is worth sharing, because, when he told me that God does not do many natural miracles anymore because we do not need them, he was taking the Bible more seriously than I think he even realized. I say that because hidden in the story of the transfiguration and in the accounts of some of the other great miracles of the Bible is the answer to our question of how come we do not need so many miracles anymore.

If we are going to discern the hidden answer, to which I have referred, in the account of the transfiguration, I need to give you a little background on what was going on in Jesus' life before it happened. According to the Gospel of Matthew, just six days before the transfiguration happened (Mark agrees, though Luke claims it was about eight days), Jesus' apostle, Peter, had been the very first person ever to proclaim Jesus as the Son of God, the Messiah. Of course, plenty of people had seen the great things that Jesus had been doing; they were aware that he was a very special gentleman. Yet until the day that Peter confessed to Jesus, "Yes, You are the Christ, the Son of the Living God (Matthew 16:16)," no one else had had the courage to say about the man Jesus that he was a God. On that fateful day somebody knew who Jesus really was.

Immediately after our beloved Peter confessed his faith in Jesus, something strange happened. Jesus made the first prediction he ever made that he would have to go to Jerusalem and die on the cross. Peter listened, and then he shouted out, "God forbid Lord! This shall never happen to you (Matthew 16:22)." Of course, Jesus got a little upset with that kind of insubordination, even if it came from the first among his apostles (see Matthew 16:18-19).

Of course, it was only natural that Peter got upset. He had just put himself on the line, stuck his neck out, by saying in front of everybody that he believed that Jesus was the Son of God. And then in the next breath Jesus says that he is going to have to die. But how could the Son of God die? Why it was as good as Jesus saying that he was not the Son of God. Who could possibly believe that Jesus was the Son of God if he had to die?

This was also a problem that Jesus and God the Father were encountering. People were just beginning to believe that Jesus was the Son of God, but it was a very fragile faith — one that could easily be shaken. Perhaps when Jesus was crucified on the cross, everyone would come to doubt his claims to such an extent, believe so firmly that it was all a hoax, that they would never hear the message of the resurrection — the real proof that Jesus was the Son of God.

Of course, the resurrection would prove to everyone that Jesus really was God's Son. However, at this point in Jesus' life, the resurrection is still several years off in the future. Consequently God faced the problem of what to do until then. To keep faith in Jesus alive he showed the disciples just how special, how extraordinary, Jesus is. He showed them by means of the miracle of the transfiguration. The miracle, then, was God's way of preparing the faithful in Jesus' time for Easter.

According to Matthew (and also according to Luke) when Jesus was transfigured, his face and clothes shone so brightly, became so white and so pure, that it almost seemed like he was a different person. It was as if he had risen from the dead. Of course, that was the whole idea behind the miracle of the transfiguration. It was intended to be a pointer to the resurrection, to Easter. And because it is a pointer to the resurrection, the miracle of transfiguration also testifies to the divine Sonship of Jesus.

There is a more general lesson for us in the miracle of the transfiguration; it is a lesson concerning how to understand all the other great miracles of Jesus (and the more modern, post-biblical ones performed by God). Just like the transfiguration, these other miracles have been performed for the same purpose — to point to the resurrection, to show that Jesus is the Son of God.

Of course, these miracles are only pointers to the resurrection. That is why we do not need them quite so urgently or in quantity any longer. Jesus and God do not want us to get too preoccupied with them. That is quite evident from all the gospels, and especially from today's text.

Immediately after the transfiguration occurred, Jesus told his disciples that under no circumstances were they to tell anyone what had happened that day until he rose from the dead (Matthew 17:9). This theme of secrecy, keeping the story of great miracles secret until the resurrection, crops up again and again in the New Testament. Jesus would perform a miracle, he might heal someone, and then he would tell everyone to keep it quiet until the resurrection.

Why did our Lord urge such secrecy? Jesus did not want people to believe in him because of those miracles. He does not want to be known as a healer, but rather as the Son of God — the man who rose from the dead. The only reason for the other miracles was to keep faith alive among his followers, to point them to the resurrection.

It is now quite evident why we do not need any more transfigurations, why we do not require many visible miracles today.

Why not? We are not in dire need of them because the greatest miracle, the one to which they all point (the miracle of Easter), has already happened. We have received all that we need in order to believe. We do not need any more.

The miracle of the transfiguration is a self-negating biblical account. We need not devote too much attention to it or to other miracles. We must avoid teaching or thinking about Jesus as a miracle worker. For the miracles are mere pointers — pointers to the miracle of God's love revealed in the resurrection.

Miracles like the ones reported in scripture still happen, less frequently and usually less visibly. Some still do happen: The miracles performed by and in the name of our modern day saints; the miracle of life, of a newborn baby; the miracle of the bread and wine becoming our Lord's body and blood; the miracle that God can use ordinary people like us to serve in his church. In these cases as well, we need to interpret such events in light of Easter. In reminding us of the new life given by Christ, these natural miracles are only truly miraculous when they serve to prepare us for that new life in Christ, to make us yearn for it. Just like the miracle of the transfiguration, these modern miracles are mere pointers to the greatest miracle — the miracle that God loves us.

[Handwritten at top: Our expectations and god's ways or god's ways and our expectations]

Lent 3 — John 4:5-26 (27-42) (C)
Lent 2 — John 4:5-26 (27-30, 39-42) (L)
Lent 3 — John 4:5-42 (RC)

The Meeting Of Marriage Partners At The Well

Jesus and his weather-beaten band of wandering disciples were still heading north and had been for some days. To some extent Jesus had decided to get out of Judea, where he had been working, in order to avoid competition with John the Baptist in that region. (John's gospel claims that the rumor was spreading all over that Jesus was baptizing more disciples than John the Baptist was.) Jesus also might have decided to head north towards familiar territory in Galilee, because the Pharisees had heard what was happening, and he may have thought that by getting away he could avoid a premature final confrontation with them early in his ministry.

The most direct route north to Galilee was through the region of Samaria. Yet a good Jew of Jesus' day would often be inclined to avoid this region. The problem with Samaria was the people who lived there. They were not good Jews. They were not pure Jews by heredity; they were Jews who had been ethnically mixed over generations of mixed marriages with the Arab race. The people of Samaria were not even faithfully practicing the Hebrew religion, but were mixing Judaism with vestiges of their earlier roots in pagan religions. Such religious practices made them (ritually) impure in the eyes of a Jew of Jesus' day. When it came to religious and social matters it was better for a Jew to avoid them.

Yet through Samaria on their way to Galilee, Jesus and his followers went. Perhaps his followers, people like you and I, wondered why the Lord would lead them into such a seedy section. Would not most of us rather just minister to people who practice their religion properly or who are socially respectable? It is easy for us to understand how Jesus' disciples might have felt. God never seems to do things our way.

At any rate, Jesus and his followers came right to the heart of the region of Samaria, to a city with a famous well called Sychar. Apparently, it had been a long, tough trip, and by the time they got near the well, about noon one day, Jesus was pretty tired. Our Lord was tired. It just reminds us again of his humanity, and how in Jesus, God has tasted all our human aches, pains and trials. God truly understands us, for he has walked in our shoes.

At any rate, Jesus sat down, rather tired, near the well that day. His disciples had proceeded into the city of Sychar to buy food for the group. And while Jesus sat there, a Samaritan woman came to the well to get water. Jesus, the Jew, met a foreign woman (a woman who was not part of an Orthodox Jewish community) at a well. For the first century Jews to whom John and the first disciples told this story, the stage was set for romance. In the stories and other forms of entertainment of the day, when a prominent Jewish boy and a foreign girl met at a well, everybody expected that a marriage between them was the next step. Yet it did not happen this time when Jesus met the Samaritan woman at the well. It did not happen. Did it? God never does the things the way we expect him to. Or does he?

The reason why first century Jews hearing the story of Jesus' meeting the Samaritan woman at the well would have presumed that a marriage was soon to follow, was that the Hebrew ethnic heritage was built on such meetings between a Jewish boy and a foreign woman (who had some bloodlines in common with the Hebrews) at a well. Moses met his eventual wife at a well. The encounter began when the daughters of the priest of Midian, Jethro (sometimes called Hobab),

Some may have thought marriage!

were trying to get water for their father's flock. Moses was at that well, fleeing from Egypt. Some shepherds began to bother the women, and Moses came to their defense, helping them water the flock. When he heard the story of Moses' kind deed, the girls' grandfather, Reuel, gave one of the girls to Moses in marriage (Exodus 2:15-21).

Jacob, the heir of Isaac (Abraham's son), also met his wife Rachel at a well. Recall that like the Midianites from whom Moses' wife descended (Genesis 25:2), the Arameans, who were the people to whom Rachel belonged, were distantly related to the Jews (Genesis 29:1ff).

The story of a Jewish boy who met his beloved foreigner through an encounter at a well had even more ancient roots, one generation further back. Jacob's father Isaac had his eventual marriage to Rebekah arranged by a meeting at a well between one of his father Abraham's servants and Rebekah. Rebekah, though not of Abraham's line and so a foreigner, was distantly related to Abraham (Genesis 24:1ff).

With these stories so much a part of their background, it is little wonder that when first century Jews heard the story of Jesus' meeting with the foreign Samaritan woman at the well, they would have expected a marriage between her and Jesus to have been the next step. Yet, of course, marriage was not on Jesus' mind. God does not usually conform to our expectations; he never does things our way. Or does he?

Besides, our beloved Jesus would not have had anything to do with such a wayward woman as the Samaritan woman he met that day at the well. Would he? After all, she had been married five times and most recently she had been living with another man. All of the foreign brides of the Old Testament patriarchs, whom I have mentioned, were virgins when they met their Jewish suitors. Not so with this Samaritan woman whom Jesus met. Our Lord would not want to have anything to do with a woman like that. Or would he? After all, God never does things our way, according to our plans. Let us return to our gospel story once again.

The Samaritan woman came to the well, and Jesus, tired as he was, asked her to give him some water. Put yourself in her shoes. God often comes to you with a request, does he not? He and his church have asked you for a lot of things over the years, have they not?

The woman's reaction was a lot like our characteristic reactions when our Lord and his church ask us to undertake a new task. "How is it that you, a Jew, ask a drink of me, a woman of Samaria?" she said to Jesus. Is that not the sort of thing we usually say when Jesus calls us? "Oh God," we say, "I am not worthy to undertake this task. Find someone else more qualified or with more time."

Jesus' response to the woman is his Word to us. He shatters all our preconceptions about him; God never does things our way. "If you knew the gift of God, and who it is that is saying to you, 'Give me a drink,' " he said, then "you would have asked him, and he would have given you living water."

Jesus seems to be saying to the woman and to us that in making the request for water, he was really inviting her and us to come to him. Is that not the way God calls us? The requests or calls he makes of us are really invitations to come to him and to be strengthened by him. Is it not the case that we usually gain more than we give when we respond to God's call or the needs of our neighbor? We gain more than we give. So often God calls us to respond to him, and we feel inadequate to the task. Yet in those moments God will set us out on these tasks only after he first serves us, only after he first feeds us with spiritual food and drink.

In a sense this is the point of our second lesson (Romans 4:1-5, 13-17 or Romans 5:1-11). Its message that we are justified by grace through faith, apart from our works, entails that we can do no good, that we cannot respond to our Lord's call until we have first been filled with the water of life, first heard the gospel of justifying grace and believed it. Jesus himself is said to have made this point elsewhere in the Gospel of John (15:5). He refers to himself as the vine and calls us believers the branches. We are urged to abide in him, to draw our sustenance from him, "for [he *(Jesus)* says] apart from me you can do nothing."

There are no good works and there is no service rendered to God unless they spring from him, unless he gives us the gift of new life. This is why Jesus made the apparently surprising move of asking the Samaritan woman to render him a service (obtaining water for him), but then telling her that she should first ask him for the true living water. Contrary to what we would ordinarily expect from God, when he calls us to service (when he asks us to work for him and his church), he is actually first giving us a gift. Keep that in mind the next time you are called to serve: You are getting something for nothing.

We are that Samaritan woman, called by Jesus, feeling unworthy of the task to which he calls us, and surprised by the generosity of his offer. What happens to her and us next? At first we, or I mean she, are hesitant about God's ability to give us this living water, this new life, that we need so badly in order to live fully. Consequently the woman questions how Jesus could provide this living water that he has promised: "Sir, you have nothing to draw with, and the well is deep; where do you get that living water (John 4:11)?"

We all have our doubts about the promises God makes. Like the Samaritan woman we question how God can really deliver on those promises. As he does with us in dealing with our doubts, Jesus responded to the woman's doubts by proclaiming his Word: ". . . the water that I shall give . . . [he says] will become in him a spring of water welling up to eternal life (John 4:14)."

As often happens to us when the Word is proclaimed, the Word overcame the woman's doubts and she confessed her faith, asking for the Lord's gift. "Sir, " she said, "Give me this water, that I may not thirst, nor come here to draw (John 4:15). "

We really are this woman from Samaria. Her experience with our Lord is also our experience. Just like he did with the woman, so God consistently shatters our expectations. He *(God)* never does things our way, or at least he rarely gives us his gifts in the manner that we could expect him to do *(them)*.

Jesus seemed to surprise the woman again. In response to her request for the living water that he alone could provide, Jesus urged the woman to go and call her husband to come. Is that not our Lord's usual manner of confounding us? We are no sooner enriched by his gifts than he sends us out to a new task. He sends us out to spread his gospel to others.

Of course, the Samaritan woman's response to Jesus' request, her reason for first hesitating to do what the Lord has asked, may seem initially odd to us. Yet in fact her response is not unlike the response we often make to our Lord when he calls us to service. And Jesus' response to her excuse is a lot like the response he makes to us in our sin.

The woman responded to Jesus' request that she summon her husband to meet Jesus and hear his word by informing Jesus that she had no husband. Oh, but Jesus saw through her excuse. He always sees through our excuses, does he not? He knows the score. Consequently he said to the woman, "You are right in saying, 'I have no husband'; for you have had five husbands, and he whom you now have is not your husband."

Jesus was dealing with a wayward woman. He was willing to offer this living water, to offer himself, to a common whore (and a Samaritan one at that). He is also willing to give himself to wayward children like you and me. For we are equally mired in sin and unfaithfulness as was that Samaritan woman.

The identification between our situation and that of the woman is made even more explicit by John in our gospel lesson when he has Jesus tell the Samaritan woman that she has had five husbands (John 4:17-18). The number of husbands she had (five) corresponds to the number of false gods (five false gods) worshiped by the Samaritans (2 Kings 17:30-34). It seems that Jesus, or at least John, wished to indicate that this woman and the Samaritans had been whoring after false gods.

Is that not the way it is with us? Are we not often whoring after our false gods, be it money, success, self-indulgence, whatever? Yet Jesus came and offered the living water to the wayward woman. He even gives it to us wayward people who surely do not deserve it. God never does things the way that we would expect him to do.

A final word: Recall that every first century Jewish hearer of this story would, at the beginning of the story, have expected Jesus to marry this woman, to marry us. For when Jewish boy met foreign girl at a well, a wedding was thought soon to follow. Yet God always confounds our expectations. He did not marry the woman. Or did he? Does he not usually carry out his promises, but just not in the way that we would expect?

John claims that after Jesus had confronted the woman with information about her waywardness and had proclaimed more of his word to her, she became firmly convinced that Jesus was the Messiah. She went into the city and proclaimed this message to the Samaritans. Not only had she received the water of life, but she had been forgiven by Jesus. She was brand new; she was a changed woman. In a sense, her relationship with Jesus had changed her, as happens in a good marriage. (You do not love in a good marriage without it changing you, right?) In a sense the Samaritan woman and Jesus had been joined in a marriage after all. It is in the same sense that we faithful should consider ourselves married to Jesus.

Martin Luther explained it so well. In 1520 he once wrote this: "The third incomparable benefit of faith is that it unites the soul with Christ as a bride united with her bridegroom. By this mystery, as the apostle teaches, Christ and the soul become one flesh [Ephesians 5:31-32]. And if they are one flesh and there is between them a true marriage . . . it follows that everything they have they hold in common, the good as well as the evil. Accordingly the believing soul can boast of and glory in whatever Christ has as though it were his own . . ."[1]

We have all that Christ has. That is why the woman and we can go out and boldly witness to Christ. We do not do it on our own. It is Christ who gives us the courage and ability, for we have all that he has. We have his courage and ability — his courage and ability to work for good and to spread the gospel to others. These gifts belong to you and me! You have them now.

Married to Christ. In an unexpected way it happened to the Samaritan woman at that well. In the same unexpected way it happened to us at the well of our baptismal waters. Of course, the idea of being married to Jesus in our baptism is not what we expected. (It is probably not what your parents or sponsors expected when they arranged your baptism.) But then, God never does things our way.

The story of Jesus and the Samaritan woman, a story about your relationship with Jesus, puts us on our guard in this Lenten season. It reminds us that the best way to prepare ourselves for Christ's coming is to be "heads-up." To be "heads-up," because God is always looking to surprise us with new ways of loving us. Are you not glad he does not do things our way? Praise God that he does not do things our way. Again and again he is always surprising you and me with his love.

Lent 4 — John 9:1-41 (C, RC)
Lent 3 — John 9:13-17, 34-39 (L)

We Must Be Blind!

What is the matter with you? Why do you never seem to understand what I say? You have ears: Why do you not hear me? Or are you blind? Can you not see what I am doing? You have eyes: Why can't you see?

Our Bible lessons for today speak directly to us. It is as if they were written with us in mind. They all make at least some reference to problems of sight and blindness — to the problem that plagues us.

"Wait a minute, Pastor! You must be kidding. These lessons cannot have much to do with our parish. To be sure, there are a few of us who do not hear as well as we once did or who could use a stronger pair of glasses. Yet none of us is blind or deaf. What does all this talk about the blind seeing have to do with us? Even if it did, you are not planning a healing service, are you Pastor?"

To the second question, I am not suggesting that we turn our parish into a congregation of charismatics. No healing services today. Yet to the first question, what does all this talk about being blind (and deaf) have to do with us, I say that it has everything to do with us.

In what way does blindness (and deafness) have to do with us? I think that to answer that question I should let you all in on a little secret about how to read the Bible. When you read the Bible or think about some of the stories in it, there is a great temptation to think, "Oh, all that is interesting, and it is wonderful to think that God could do this for people long ago; yet it does not have much to do with me" Certainly this is a temptation. However, what we really must do if we want to be open to hear God's Word in the scriptures is to be prepared to locate ourselves in the stories. We should seek to find ourselves in the biblical accounts, regarding the characters in the Bible to whom God is speaking and interacting as representing you and me. We come to learn a little bit about who we are by identifying ourselves with these people.[1]

This way of reading scripture entails identification with the blind man whom Jesus healed. You remember the story. A blind man had been brought to Jesus on the sabbath day, and Jesus healed him by putting some clay over his eyes. The Pharisees, who were some of Jesus' main tormentors, heard about what had happened, and they really grilled this poor fellow whom Jesus had healed. They grilled him first about the nature of the miracle. Then they made a lot of accusations against Jesus for working on the sabbath, which was, of course, a sin for the ancient Jews. Just the same, the man whom Jesus healed stood his ground. "This is a great man," he said. "He is a prophet (John 9:17)." And eventually he took his lumps for saying it.

What courage we have here! The man was harassed terribly for his brave defense of Jesus. The Pharisees questioned him and his parents about whether he was actually blind; they tried to show that the miracle was just a fake. Yet the man stood his ground (even though his parents backed away and let him take all of the heat). He even went so far as to confess that Jesus was from God (John 9:33). Of course, he paid the price. The Pharisees cast him out of the local synagogue.

This man whom Jesus healed certainly demonstrated an appropriate gratitude to Jesus, a true faith, did he not? In his faith he teaches us something about ourselves. Like him, we have all been touched by the good news of Jesus Christ. In a way it has healed us from our blindness, has it not? This is Paul's point in our epistle lesson for today (Ephesians 5:8-14). We are not in darkness; we are not spiritually blind anymore. We know everything that is necessary; we know that our salvation depends on Christ. We are not blind. Much like that blind man in our gospel text we are witnessing to our gratitude and our faith by our attendance here this Sunday morning.

To be sure, there is a lot that we can learn about ourselves from the blind man in this morning's story. Perhaps we can learn a lot more than we think. Listen to the rest of the story, and see if you do not gain further insights about who you are.

Immediately after standing up to the Pharisees, telling them what a great man Jesus was, and even enduring the Pharisees' chastisement, the blind man (now no longer blind) runs into Jesus again. Jesus asked the man, "Do you believe in the Son of Man (John 9:35)?" The man looked at Jesus, even after having been healed by him, and he said, "And who is he, sir, that I may believe in him (John 9:36)?" Jesus answered, "You have seen him, and it is he who speaks to you (John 9:37)."

Imagine! Imagine that! Here the answer is standing right in front of this fellow, the Son of Man. He has been healed by Jesus. He has experienced his great power. The man who was healed can now see, his eyes are working fine, and he is still acting as if he were blind. This man certainly acts an awful lot like you and I do.

Week after week, you and I assemble in this building. We come together to hear the good news of Jesus Christ. Hopefully we hear a little bit of it on our own through personal prayers and family devotions. Yes, we hear a lot of the good news of Jesus Christ. But is it making a difference in our lives? Is it?

Week after week, we come together as the family of God. In fact our Christian community (the church) is not just a Sunday thing; it exists all week long. Its purpose, a primary purpose of the church, is to give support to Christians, to be a fellowship in which we can lean on each other's shoulders when things are tough (1 Corinthians 12:12-26). This is the purpose of the church. We all know this. Yet it seems like in any church, not just in our parish but elsewhere, too, you seem to find people more critical, more likely to stab others in the back, than among any other group of people. Consequently, the church does just the opposite of what God intended it to do. We must be blind — or deaf.

Time and time again we have heard the good news of Jesus urge us to live by faith. How many times have we heard Jesus ask us to consider the lilies of the field, how they do not sow or toil, and yet how God provides for them (Matthew 6:28ff; Luke 12:27ff)?" How many times have we been urged not to be too anxious about the future? How many times? Yet, we keep on worrying about tomorrow. We pile up more and more — more money, more things. We do not even seem to have enough. We need more — for security. It is as if we had never heard Jesus' parable.

How about the good news? How about the good news that, because of Jesus Christ, God has forgiven us, that he loves us just the way we are — that we do not have to earn his love? That means that we are lovable. We cannot be all bad. What other people think does not have to matter so much anymore.

Yet no matter how many times you and I have heard it, it just does not seem to sink in — not really. To be sure, we all believe that God loves us. Yet, too often we do not take the next step. We do not believe that, if God the Creator loves us the way we are, then we must be quite lovable. No, we do not live our lives in that kind of confidence. Instead, you and I become too preoccupied with what other people might think of us. Sometimes this unfaithfulness on our part takes the form of an "I can't do that; I'm not good enough." Other times we wind up doing things that we really do not want to do, simply because other people think that we should do it, because it is the thing to do.

Again and again the good news of God's love for us and the self-confidence that goes with it comes our way. It comes to us in God's Word. We can see it, even taste it, in the sacrament of Holy communion. Yet it is often like we never "heard" about this Word, for all the genuine self-confidence it gives to us. No, we are just like the blind man whom Jesus cured. We have our eyes, but we cannot see. We cannot seem to recognize God's love and what it could mean for our lives. We cannot recognize that love, even though it is right in front of our eyes.

The prophet Isaiah (in our first lesson, Isaiah 42:19-20) says it all: "Who is blind but my servant, or deaf as my messenger whom I send? Who is blind as my dedicated one, or blind as the servant of the Lord? [Israel] you see many things, but do not observe them . . ."

We see many things in our daily lives, but really do not observe them. The secret to life, everything that we need in order to live happy and fulfilled lives is right here. It is here in this book (the Bible). It is here at the altar on every Communion Sunday. It even comes from this pulpit, at least every once-in-a-while (whenever the Holy Spirit uses the preacher who stands here). Yes, the key to a full, happy life is all here.

Isaiah is really correct. We have seen so much; yet it has not meant enough to us in our lives. We have the eyes that we need in order to see and the ears that we need in order to hear. Yet we have not seen and heard — not really.

Jesus said the same thing at the very end of our gospel lesson's story about the healing of the blind man. Some Pharisees were overhearing Jesus' dialogue with the blind man whom he had healed, and Jesus said to them, "If you were blind, you would have no guilt; but now that you say, 'We see,' your guilt remains (John 9:41)." We say that we can see, but in actual fact we do not notice all that God has given us. We really must be blind!

Listen all you deaf and blind people: There really is good news! God is still eager to save. Prepare yourself for his coming into your life. He is already present. It is all here; the secret to the good and happy life is already manifest and present. Consequently let us wake up and start grabbing hold. God is eager. It is like the old Christian hymn that Paul sang in our

second lesson says: "Awake, O sleeper, and arise from the dead, and Christ shall give you light (Ephesians 5:14)."
 Christ shall give you light.

Lent 4
Matthew 20:17-28 (L)
Competition In The Kingdom?

Jesus and his faithful band had begun their final journey to Jerusalem; it was the last trip that they would take together. Along the way Jesus told them again that he would be condemned to death by the authorities, he would die, but would be raised on the third day. It would happen to him on this very trip to Jerusalem, he said. This was the third time that Jesus had made this prophecy in the presence of his followers. Yet this time, according to Matthew, there was no reaction of shock or disbelief by the disciples, like there had been the other times that Jesus had foretold his death (Matthew 16:22; Matthew 17:23). Perhaps they were just becoming accustomed to living with such a horrible thought. Perhaps they were just becoming hardened. Or perhaps they were beginning to believe it.

Is not that the way it is with us? At first we are stunned by the shocking news. We hurt with the one afflicted. But eventually we become hardened and not so sensitive. We really are fickle people.

Perhaps the disciples were not so fickle according to Matthew's account. Perhaps their silence was an indication that they had begun to come to terms with God's will. Perhaps their silence was a testimony to their faith in God and their trust in the wisdom of his ways. Perhaps. Yet then, almost immediately, such faith lapsed into incredible ignorance and egocentrism.

Is that not the way it is with us? One moment we sing God's praises and seek with all our heart to walk in his ways. The next moment, or even as we think we are walking in faith, it is all marred by our egocentricity and our yearning for the acclaim of the crowd. At least this is what happened to two of Jesus' disciples and their mother. Here is the story:

James and John, two sons of Zebedee, were among Jesus' 12 disciples. In fact, they were prominent among his disciples. According to Matthew, they were among the first disciples whom Jesus called (responding right after our Lord had called Peter and Andrew). Like their father, they had been fishermen (Matthew 4:18-22; cf. Mark 1:16-18; Luke 5:1-11). Yet they seemed to have a prominent place among the other disciples. When Matthew lists the disciples, the brothers are at the top of the list (Matthew 10:1-4; Mark 3:14-19; Luke 6:13-16). Along with Peter, James and John were the three disciples whom Jesus wanted with him when he struggled with his anxieties in prayer at the Garden of Gethsemane (Matthew 26:37; Mark 14-33). Some believe, at least according to John's own version of the gospel, that John was the beloved disciple to whom Jesus actually entrusted his mother as he was dying (John 19:25-27).

No doubt about it, these two sons of Zebedee were truly devoted to Jesus. It is believed that James met a martyr's death after being the early church's first missionary to Spain. And John continued to carry on a ministry with Peter in Jerusalem after Jesus' ascension into heaven (Acts 3:1-4; 8:14). Do you and I not try to live as faithfully in our own way?

Yet on the day when our gospel lesson took place, this sort of faith was not much in evidence. We and the two of them approached Jesus along with their mother. Their mother was herself no insignificant figure among Jesus' followers. Although there is some disclarity about her name (it may have been Salome), it is clear in Matthew and in other gospels that she accompanied Jesus to the very end.¹ She was present at the crucifixion (Matthew 27:56; Mark 15:40-41). She may have even seen the Risen Lord on that first Easter (Mark 16:1ff). The woman had, or was to receive so much glory. Yet it was not enough; she wanted more. She asked Jesus to give her two sons the highest place possible in the kingdom. Is not that kind of discontent, that sort of lust for recognition and reputation, the way it is with us?

We faithful followers of Jesus are never fully content, are we? Of course, when we are not content with all that has been given us, we are not being faithful. Yet at any rate, it is true, we are not content with the rich honor and glory that God has bestowed upon us.

In our baptisms, we have been made people of God. What an unspeakable honor has been bestowed on us! The words of Paul which were once the words of the prophet Hosea ring in our ears: "Those who were not my people I will call 'my people' . . . (Romans 9:25; cf. Hosea 1-10; 2:23)"

God has made us his people. What more could you and I want? Yet so very often we members of his church want more.

There are still some parts of the world, some parts of this country, in which your social standing is helped by the role you play or the office you hold in a congregation. In such settings, people lust for positions of power and influence. Perhaps it is like that in this parish, too.

I am reminded of a story about a church in the South. An officer in that congregation once chided the pastor for failing to have the congregation's officers (his name and the name of his father) included in every congregational mailing. The church officer's rationale for his request was that he felt that the leaders deserved the recognition. But the officers' problem also was related to their failure to understand the meaning of their baptism and Christian service. Is ours a congregation like that one?

In that parish the leaders' lust for power and recognition created hostility, real anger among hard-working members of the congregation who had not quite arrived in the inner elite.

This group resented the leadership. Of course, one would have expected such a reaction. Even the disciples reacted that way to the pushiness of the mother of James and John. Matthew tells us that when the other 10 heard the pitch for a higher standing on the part of the mother of James and John they got angry (Matthew 20:24). It is just a human reaction. It is evident that by such competition and jockeying for position, the Body of Christ is fractured. Beware my friends, the next time that you seek to exert undue influence and yearn for power in the church.

Of course it is not just the laity who fall prey to the competition and power syndrome of James, John, and their mother. Clergy in the congregation can tell us about the power politics and influence-peddling of the ecclesiastical institution's ordained leaders. We can tell you about the clergy success track, how leadership is often measured by the criteria of whom you have climbed over and whether your colleagues admire your accomplishments and position. The reaction of Jesus' disciples to the competition game for status and position tells us a lot about the church today. That game is all too often played among us. We need to prepare for our Lord's coming in this Lenten season by confessing our sin.

Of course, leadership positions in the church and the temptation to play power games with them may not be everybody's hang-up. Yet the competition game which occurred that day among Jesus' disciples points to a dynamic which has broad implications for us in late 20th century American society. One prominent social analyst put it well. As a description of the modern American mind-set, he wrote: "Today men seek the kind of approval that applauds not their actions but their personal attributes. They wish to be not so much esteemed as admired. They crave not fame but the glamor and excitement of celebrity. They want to be envied rather than respected . . . the successful bureaucrat survives not by appealing to the authority of his office but by establishing a pattern of upward movement, cultivating upwardly mobile superiors, and administering 'homeopathetic doses of humiliation' to those he leaves behind in his ascent to the top."[2]

Is this not the dynamic that lies behind the interactions that the disciples had with each other on the day that the mother of James and John tried to get them a special place in the kingdom? Our gospel lesson gets us in touch with one of the core social dynamics and problems of our day. Do you not find your life illumined by the story? How often are you striving to get to the top of your company, to find a place in your community or circle, over someone else by means of promoting yourself and your image? We are all guilty. Paul hits the nail on the head in our second lesson today. He talks about how God has set us free from the law. To live under the law, to try to prove your worth by what you do, will only lead you to things of the flesh (Romans 8:1-10). That is what happens to us when we become preoccupied with promoting ourselves and our image at someone else's expense. When we believe that way, we are being preoccupied with things of the flesh. We are living under the law, because we are trying to prove our worth by what we do. The outcome of it all is hopelessness and death.

Yet Paul reminds us that we have been set free from all that. Christ is in us, and we are alive. The same promise is made in a veiled way in our first lesson. God promises to raise us up on the third day. The suggestion is a pointer to Easter where God makes us new (Hosea 6:1). We do not need to achieve or to compete with our neighbors at their expense. God has set us free and given us the marks of greatness. He has made you and me his people.

Referring back to an earlier comment he had made to James, John, and their mother about his passion (the cup he would have to drink [Matthew 20:25]), Jesus referred them all again to the cross. ". . . whoever would be great among you must be your servant, and whoever would be first among you must be your slave; even as the Son of Man came not to be served but to serve, and to give his life as a ransom for many (Matthew 20:27-28).''

If you want to be great in the kingdom, Jesus says, you are someone who is always giving up your life for someone else. That is what the cross is all about: Giving up your life for someone else (cf. Galatians 6:14; Matthew 16:24).

Bearing the cross, however, is not a task laid on us; it is not something we have to do. It is part of our baptismal inheritance. In baptism we took on the life of the cross, whatever happened to Jesus became ours. We were given an inclination to live the life that Jesus did — a life of constantly denying ourselves (dying to self) for the sake of our neighbor (Colossians 2:12; Romans 6:3ff).[3] Jesus says in our gospel lesson that such a lifestyle is the true mark of greatness (Matthew 20:26). Do you not see the point? We are great already. Baptism has given us all that we will ever need; nothing could be more estimable or admirable. We are God's people! And that makes us servants of Christ and our neighbor.

Of course, the role of a servant is not all that appealing to the crowd caught up in worldly things. We in the church are drawn to the idea at first. We want a "hassle-free Christianity." We are reminded once again that God never gives us what we expect. I am reminded of those officers in that southern parish who wanted their names on every parish publication. They also objected to every effort to establish standards for membership and baptismal instruction in that parish, because it would create hassles and no one wants that. They were too caught up in worldly power games to hear the word of the cross and its invitation to self-denial.

Are we not inclined to think that way too sometimes? The voice of the crowd lures us away to a quest for approval and glamour at the expense of others. Yet, Jesus tells us that true greatness lies in denying ourselves in order to serve God and our neighbor.

This sort of lifestyle, bearing the cross of self-denial, will tear you away from your preoccupation with the things of this world. It is the church's and God's "no" to the "me-first," "give me approval and acclaim, admire me" ethos of contemporary social trends. In face of these trends, what we need is a strong dose of the cross. (Prepare yourself; it is already manifest.) Christ has already laid that one on us in our baptisms. The mark of greatness (the cross) is already on you. Christians, go with courage and do as God intends.

Lent 5
John 11:(1-6) 17-45 (C)
John 11:1-53 (L)
John 11:1-45 (RC)

The Resurrection Is Freedom

We have all lived through the death of a loved one. We have all ached when someone we dearly love has passed away. We have all wondered about what comes next, and fretted about our own death. In our gospel story for today we find Jesus dealing with those experiences. And together with Lazarus, Jesus (along with our other Bible lessons) shows us what comes next after sin and death. He does not just show it; he gives it. What he gives is freedom given through love. That is what comes next when the new life is given, when death and sin are conquered. Freedom given through love is what awaits us on the other side of death. Let us hear the story.

Jesus certainly loved the dying man and his family. When Mary and Martha (Lazarus' sisters) first came to tell Jesus about their brother's illness, they did it by telling Jesus, "Lord, he whom you love is ill (John 11:3)." Jesus did indeed love Lazarus. The Bible tells us about the close bond he had with the whole family. Thus the writer of this story, John (11:5), writes: "Now Jesus loved Martha and her sister and Lazarus." Jesus loved them.

Jesus' love for that family was not just a matter of words, a kind of polite sentiment we sometimes express concerning acquaintances. This was a passionate love. Thus after learning that Lazarus was severely ill, Jesus concluded his business in the region of Perea (Jesus always conducts his business deliberately in John's gospel; also see John 2:4, 24; 12:1) and he went back to Judea to be with his friends. He loved Lazarus and his sisters that much that he changed his plans for them. In fact, Jesus loved them so much that he was willing to risk his life for Lazarus, because the disciples thought it would be better for Jesus to stay out of Lazarus' home region. The Jews who lived there, you see, were very hostile to Jesus (John 11:8ff). But Jesus did not care; he loved Lazarus that much.

Then when Jesus learned from Lazarus' sisters that Lazarus was dead, and when he saw Mary and all of Lazarus' friends crying, Jesus was troubled. When he saw where they had laid Lazarus' body, even Jesus wept. The tears he cried must have been genuine, not just polite tears. For the Jews who were around the tomb who saw him cry responded: "See how he loved him [Lazarus] (John 11:36)!" Yes, Jesus really knows what it is to grieve over the loss of someone you love. God really understands us. He has lived through our trials.

It is a little easier to love Jesus when we recognize how he has walked in our shoes. A little easier to love him when we see how much and how deeply he loves. Martin Luther said it so well in a sermon that he preached in 1518 on this very gospel story. About the love that Jesus showed Lazarus, Lazarus' family, and us, Luther said: "Let us therefore learn to know from the gospel how kindly Christ deals with us; then we shall without a doubt love him and avoid sinning and so see everything in a different light."[1]

Experiencing the love of Christ like we can in this gospel story of the raising of Lazarus from the dead makes you love Christ all the more. Luther says that it helps us to avoid sin and see everything in a new light. What is that new light in which we see things?

Of course, on the surface the answer to that question is obvious. We Christians see both death and life in light of the resurrection. Jesus brought Lazarus back to life from death. And not just Lazarus. Death will not have the final word with you and me. We have Jesus' word on it: "I am the resurrection and the life [he says]; he who believes in me, though he die, yet shall he live, and whoever lives and believes in me shall never die (John 11:25-26)." The promise of the resurrection and the new life that goes with it are ours.

Of course, when we talk this way about the resurrection we are inclined to think of it as something that lies ahead of us somewhere in the distant future. The story of the raising of Lazarus throws new light on that matter. After all, Lazarus' resurrection was not far off in the future. It happened that very day that Jesus came to him — just four days after his death. Resurrection and the new life that comes with it is a present reality!

Think about that point for a moment. This idea that the new life given in the resurrection is already available to the faithful is a central (though too often overlooked) theme in Jesus' preaching. Think how often in the first three (synoptic) gospels Jesus proclaims that the kingdom of God (the new order of things) "is at hand (Matthew 4:17; Mark 1:15; Luke 11:20; 17:21)."[2] John seems to make the same point in his representation of Jesus in our gospel story today. When Jesus finally got to Bethany (Lazarus' hometown) and learned from Lazarus' sister Martha that Lazarus was dead, then (according to John) Jesus said to her, "Your brother will rise again (John 11:23)." Martha responded (sort of like we would), "I know that he will rise again in the resurrection at the last day (John 11:24)."

Martha sounds like us modern Christians; we believe in the resurrection, in the new life, but we think of it as something far off in the future. However, Jesus responded to her and to us (in our thinking about the resurrection being far off in the future), "I am the resurrection and the life; he who believes in me, though he die, yet shall he live, and whoever lives and believes in me shall never die (John 11:25-26)."

The resurrection is already present in Jesus. We already have the resurrection (the new life) when we have him present among us. In fact, when Jesus is present, in an ultimate or final sense, death is no more! The new life is given! If Jesus is the resurrection and the life, then to have him present is to have the resurrection and the new life now in the present. And then to make his point that the resurrection is already present (that we do not have to wait for it at some far off point in the future) Jesus proceeds to raise Lazarus from the dead. (It all pointed to his resurrection on Easter which would not be far off.)

Our gospel story to this point answers the question with which we began this sermon — the question of what comes next after death. The resurrection and the new life come immediately for those who are in Christ. We do not have to wait for them. (In a real sense death has not ultimately separated us from our loved ones. They are still with us in the sense that God is caring for them now, like he is caring for us. Consequently, whenever Jesus comes to us he brings our loved ones with him.) That is the different light in which we can view the sufferings, sins and the evil that are in the world. Suffering, sin and evil do not have the final word in our lives, or even in the lives of our loved ones who are gone. Sin, suffering, and even death, do not have the final word.

What is the nature of the new life, of the resurrection, that is already ours? All three of our Bible lessons for today give us some clues. First, we have some hints about the nature of the new life of resurrection right there in our story about Lazarus.

Jesus had gone to the tomb of Lazarus, a cave with a stone on it. And Jesus commanded that the stone be removed. (We have another reminder of Jesus' own resurrection, of the stone that the angels rolled away on that first Easter [John 20:1; Luke 24:2; Mark 16:4; Matthew 28:2].) Lazarus' sister Martha noted how after four days the body would smell if they removed the stone (John 11:39). But after the stone was rolled away (Jesus had promised that they would see the glory of God if they believed [John 11:40]), then Jesus proceeded to thank the Father, explained to him his aims, and then he called out with a loud voice: "Lazarus, come out (John 11:41-43)." John tells us what happened next: "The dead man came out, his hands and feet bound with bandages, and his face wrapped with a cloth. Jesus said to them, 'Unbind him, and let him go.' (John 11:44)."

Back to our gospel story, John says that Lazarus came out of the tomb bound with bandages and wrapped with a cloth. (This seems to have been the embalming practice of the day.) Yet Jesus wanted him loosened, unbound. In view of the connotation of the use of this term in Greek, the connotation that unbinding or loosening from something was an unbinding from sin, does John want us to understand the bandages and cloth wrapped around Lazarus in death as symbolizing sin? In raising Lazarus from the dead, in giving him new life, Jesus was unbinding or loosening Lazarus from sin! Lazarus really could not begin to live that new life Jesus had given him until Lazarus was first loosened and freed from sin.

It makes sense, does it not? The Bible (especially Paul) clearly associates death with sin (Romans 6:23; 5:12, 17). The conquest of one is the conquest of the other. Jesus conquered death that day when he raised Lazarus from the dead. He also loosed Lazarus from sin.

Lazarus was given a new life that day at the tomb. It is rather like the new life that God gave you in your baptism (Romans 6:4-11). The new life that Jesus gave Lazarus was a life loosed from bondage, loosed from the bandages and the cloth that bound him in death, loosed from the sin that trapped him and us.

All of our Bible lessons for today make this point. In our first lesson, God used the prophet Ezekiel to bring the people of Israel back to life from the dead. God gives the people and us new life, returns them to their own land (delivering them and us from the exile and bondage we were under). He promises to put his Spirit within them and us (Ezekiel 37:14). Earlier God made it clear that this giving of the Spirit, this new life that he gives Israel and us, involves a cleansing from sin, the infusion of a new heart in the faithful (Ezekiel 36:25-29). The new life that God gives us sets us free from sin and the fear of death, free to serve him anew.

Our second lesson from Paul's letter to the Romans makes the same point. Paul says it explicitly at the beginning of the chapter from which we are reading. He claims to be talking about the new life which Christ has given the faithful. Here is what he says: "For the law of the Spirit of life in Christ Jesus has set me free from the law of sin and death (Romans 8:2)."

Free from sin and death. That is what the new life is all about. Paul makes the same point in our lesson. He writes: "If the Spirit of him who raised Jesus from the dead dwells in you, he who raised Christ Jesus from the dead will give life to your mortal bodies also through his Spirit which dwells in you (Romans 8:11)."

God has given us life. This new life is tied to the resurrection of Christ. As we have seen, this new life is a life of freedom — freedom from sin and evil, freedom from being anxious and troubled about our death and the death of our loved ones.

Paul in our second lesson, Ezekiel in our first lesson, and our gospel story about the raising of Lazarus add one more item to our reflections on the resurrection and the new life. Resurrection, new life and freedom are not just realities still to be manifested in the distant future. The new life and resurrection are happening now. They happen whenever Jesus Christ is present among us, because, as he said to Martha in our gospel story for today, "I am the resurrection and the life (John 11:25)." Whenever you believe in him, the new life, the reality of the resurrection, is yours. Hear Jesus' words again to Martha: ". . . he who believes in me, though he die, yet shall he live, and whoever lives and believes in me shall never die (John 11:25-26)."

When you believe in Jesus, you have the assurance that death, sin, evil and temptation will never have the final word in your life. You and I have been set free from such anxieties! The resurrection and the new life are a life of freedom from sin and from all the anxieties about what comes next (cf. Matthew 6:25-34; Luke 12:22-28). Thanks to the love that he had for Lazarus and his family, God is giving us new life, the reality of the resurrection, which sets us free.

Lent is a season of preparation — a time to get ready for Easter. The message of this fifth Sunday in Lent is that we are wise to be prepared for this new life of the resurrection all of the time. It is well for us to be on our guard every moment, for at any time the new life and the freedom that goes with it could be entering your life.

Ever feel like you had a new lease on life? Ever feel like all the cares, anxieties, and temptations you were facing had been lifted, that you were free? Ever feel like the loved ones you had lost really had not finally been taken from you? Ever feel like you had a chance for a fresh start? In those cases, you were experiencing a resurrection no less dramatic and miraculous than what happened to Lazarus. Those moments when you had a fresh start, when you were truly freed, were God's gifts of love to you.

Heads up, people, those wonderful, freeing moments of the new life given by God out of his love for you are offered so often by our Lord, often in the most unexpected places. Heads up, or you will miss them! Be prepared for the miracle of the resurrection! That miracle, the miracle of the new life that God wants to give you, is always at hand!

Sunday Of The Passion
Matthew 26:14—27:66 (C, RC)
Matthew 26:1—27:66 (L)

The Road To The Cross

Passion Sunday, the whole story of the dastardly plots and betrayals that brought Jesus to the cross, lies before us. You know the story well. It is filled with a number of subplots, all of which provide insights about the kind of people that we are and how our sins nailed Jesus to the cross. We see how the disciples (especially Judas and Peter, as well as the sons of Zebedee), each in his own way, failed our Lord. In similar ways we have failed him.

We hear the story of our Lord's courage, his love of peace. We see him practice what he preaches when he renounces the use of violence to save himself from arrest (Matthew 26:51-56).

We see Jesus before the Sanhedrin (the highest court and council of ancient Judaism) and observe the schemes of the chief priests, the Pharisees and the Jewish elders (esp. see Matthew 26:57-75). More of that later. Their schemes, in an unfortunate, equally heinous way, are our schemes, too. Yet, it all comes to a climax when Jesus is brought before Pilate. What ultimately brought Jesus to the cross were the schemes of the Jewish religious establishment and Pilate's cowardly judgment. Thus, let us begin at that final point.

You know the story as well as I do: Pilate and his wife would have liked to release Jesus (Matthew 27:14, 19, 23).

Matthew (and Mark) says that Pilate realized that the chief priests, the Jewish authorities, were envious of Jesus (Matthew 27:18; cf. Mark 15:10). In response, Pilate tried to spare Jesus by offering the crowd a choice between Jesus and (according to Matthew's version) a "notable [or notorious] prisoner" named Barabbas (who may also have been named Jesus — Jesus Barabbas) (Matthew 27:15-17). Yet, the chief priests and the Jewish elders tried to stir up the crowd, to get the crowd to select Barabbas as the one to free. The scheme of the Jewish authorities worked (Matthew 27:19-20).

"Pilate said to them, 'Then what shall I do with Jesus who is called Christ?' They all said, 'Let him be crucified.' And [Pilate] said [to the crowd], 'Why, what evil has he done?' But they shouted all the more. 'Let him be crucified' (Matthew 27:21-23)." Crucify him.

"So when Pilate saw that he was gaining nothing, but rather that a riot was beginning, he took water and washed his hands before the crowd, saying, 'I am innocent of this man's blood, see to it yourself.' And all the people answered, 'His blood be on us and on our children!' Then he released for them Barabbas, and having scourged Jesus, delivered him to be crucified (Matthew 27:24-26)."

It is not a pretty story. Yet it is a story full of insights about the nature of our sin. In fact, this is a story that we need to tell. We need to tell it because the story uncovers an element of sin that American Christianity, because of some of our history in this country, has too often overlooked. The story of the sentence of Jesus testifies to us that sin is not just an individual's affair; sin is a social problem. In fact, it was social sin, the sin that permeates our social structures, which finally and ultimately brought Jesus to the cross.

What do I mean by "social sin?" By social sin, I refer to the reality of evil that is bigger than you and I are as individuals. I refer to the perversion of the institutions of society in such a way that these institutions, though created to serve human beings, become agents of sin, evil and harm. In our century, the most obvious example of social sin is evident in the social structures of National Socialism and the Third Reich in Germany during World War II. One also thinks of the South African apartheid system. But let us not forget the way in which the runaway economic system of pre-Depression America caused untold suffering to the American people, or the way in which the international capitalist system of multi-national corporations causes many to suffer inhuman working conditions and exploits the poor today. We could cite other examples.

At any rate, this is what I mean when I speak of social sin. Social sin happens when society's institutions become the agents of sin and evil, so that these institutions corrupt basically decent people and make people like you and me to do their bidding to work evil.

Such is the nature of social sin. Yet we have not said enough about it in the churches of this country (not following the insights of liberation theology in Latin America). We have been too much inclined merely to dwell on the sins of individuals — on our own or on other people's misdeeds. It is for these sins, we say, that Jesus died.

Perhaps our reluctance to consider social sin has to do with our good old American hang-up about not mixing religion and politics. For if we criticize social sin, the fear is that the church is inevitably involving itself in criticizing the political structures. And we must not do that!

It may be that we have gotten to the root of American Christianity's reluctance about dealing with social sin. Yet I do not believe that we can remain silent about such sin any longer, at least not if we take seriously the gospel's accounts of Jesus' road to the cross. For as I noted previously, according to Matthew (and the other gospel writers), it was the sin that permeated the social structures of Jesus' day that finally brought him to the cross. Matthew seems to be using the story of Jesus' condemnation as a way of condemning social sin. Let us consider the story in more detail.

Social sin; the lust for power; the determination to maintain control and to remain in power, no matter what compromises we need to make; apathy — the kind of apathy that leads us to go along with the crowd and with our leaders, even if they are not doing the right thing. We are all guilty of such sin. Pilate was also guilty, as were the chief priests and the elders and the crowd. We all sentenced Jesus to death.

Matthew's version of the story is perhaps not as kind to Pontius Pilate as is Luke's version (see Luke 23:20, 22). Yet even in Matthew, as in Mark's version, it is clear that Pilate (and certainly his wife) does not think that Jesus is guilty of the Jewish Sanhedrin's accusations. In fact, Pilate seems to have tried to get Jesus off the hook by offering the crowd a choice between Jesus and Barabbas the prisoner. Because, according to Matthew, "[Pilate] knew that it was out of envy that they [the chief priests and the elders] had delivered him [Jesus] up (Matthew 27:18)."

No, Pilate, along with his wife, knew right from wrong on the matter (Matthew 27:19). Yet, Pilate failed to do the right thing. Of course you cannot blame him too much. (At least that is one argument on his behalf.) He was under all kinds of terrible pressures.

To be the Roman governor of Israel in the time of Jesus was no easy task. The Jews of the day were nationalistic and many were religious fanatics. It would be sort of like a foreigner trying to govern Iran today. No, Rome and Pilate might have been in charge of Israel in Jesus' day. However, they had a delicate balancing act to do if they were to keep things under control and peaceful. Consequently, if enough Jews were against Jesus, the thing for Pilate to do was to play to the crowd — to give them what they wanted (even if Pilate knew that Jesus did not deserve the punishment).

Keep the crowd happy, even if it is at the expense of your integrity and commitments. That was Pilate's formula; that was his sin. (Contrary to what he wanted to do, he really could not wash his hands of this sin [Matthew 27:24].) It is your sin and my sin, too, is it not?

However, it is not just Pilate who was complying in such social sin, who was concerned to maintain the status quo of evil social institutions. The chief priests and the rest of the religious establishment of Jesus' day wanted him put away. According to Matthew (26:47ff), it was the chief priests and the elders who were involved in first capturing Jesus in Gethsemane. They engineered the betrayal by Judas Iscariot (Matthew 26:14-16). They and the scribes engineered the trial before the Sanhedrin (Matthew 26:57ff). They delivered Jesus to Pilate (Matthew 27:1ff). And they stirred up the crowd (Matthew 27:20)!

Why did they do it? Social sin was involved. The quest for power. Matthew 21 makes that very clear. When Jesus first came to Jerusalem, he cleansed the temple of the moneychangers and proceeded to do some miracles. Apparently, a number of people, notably children, were impressed. But the chief priests and the scribes were indignant about it (Matthew 21:12-15).

Next came other verbal confrontations with the religious establishment. After a time Jesus returned to the temple to teach, and according to Matthew, at least one parable Jesus taught was perceived by the religious establishment as being told at their expense. It was then that they resolved to arrest Jesus, and they only refrained at that time for fear of inciting Jesus' supporters (especially Matthew 21:45-46). Finally, after several more confrontations, in which the established leaders were made to look bad by Jesus in front of others (Matthew 22:15ff, 23-24), our gospel (at the beginning of Chapter 26) tells us that "the chief priests and the elders of the people gathered in the palace of the high priest, who was called Caiaphas, and took counsel together in order to arrest Jesus by stealth and kill him (Matthew 26:3-4)." The plan of the religious establishment to put Jesus away seems to have had its origins in jealousy over the influence that Jesus was having on the crowd in Jerusalem.

What else is this but social sin and the thirst for power and influence? The chief priests and the elders, the religious establishment, were afraid that Jesus was taking away their power and influence. Thus, in order to maintain their power, in order to maintain the religious establishment, they moved to put Jesus away.

Have you never done it? In order to keep your favorite institution running just the way you like it, have you ever helped ease the trouble-maker out? Have you ever hurt someone in the name of your favorite institution? Have you ever "done someone dirty" in order to keep your important position on the job or in the community? Not so quick with your denial. If you have ever held an office that you cared about in this congregation, in this community or on your job, you have done it! I have done it. Our yearning for power and influence, like that of the Jewish religious establishment of Jesus' day, nailed him to the cross.

Perhaps you do not think that you are guilty of the dynamics of social sin that we have thus far explored. However, you will surely discover yourself in the sinful passivity of the crowd that gathered around Jesus and Pilate. That crowd had a chance to free Jesus. They could have chosen him instead of Barabbas as the man whom they wanted to set free. This was, after all, no doubt the same crowd that just five days earlier, on Palm Sunday, had cheered Jesus wildly as he entered Jerusalem (Matthew 21:8-9). Yet more recently, many in this crowd had been so convinced that Jesus was a prophet that they had made it impossible for the chief priests and the Pharisees to arrest him (Matthew 21:46). And now, fickle people, they proclaimed, "Let him be crucified (Matthew 27:22, 23)."

Why had the crowd changed its mind? Because everyone else was calling for the crucifixion. And why did they all want it? Matthew says because the chief priests and the rest of the religious leadership stirred them up (Matthew 27:20).

Too often, is it not that way with us? Are we not inclined to "go with the flow," to let the latest American social convention or trend dictate our actions, decisions and values? Is it not true that too often we let the high priests, the leaders, of American social convention stir us up in determining the things that we do? Do we not make our purchases, determine our values, form our dreams on the basis of what the high priests of the American media proclaim?

Certainly, the younger generations among us are guilty of such behavioral patterns. However, even those of you more set in your ways have been susceptible to such influences. Are not your values, your way of doing retirement, or your image of the good life shaped by the American cultural agenda — the "American dream" (no matter if that dream has been exploiting the poor in our nation and throughout the world)?

We really are like that Jewish crowd which followed Jesus. How often, like that crowd, have we refrained from standing up for what we know was right, and instead gone along with the flow, along with everyone else — gone along with everybody else because we did not want to rock the boat. It happens in this congregation sometimes, does it not?

I refer once again here to social sin. It manifests itself whenever we let evil social institutions and unethical trends go their own way even though, in our hearts, we know that they are wrong. Our gospel lesson from Matthew is emphatically clear on this point. It was such social sin that nailed Jesus to the cross.

It is evident that sin is not just the transgressions of an individual — not just your sin and my sin, but the sin of our institutions and the lust for power that we have about finding a place or protecting our place in these institutions. How can the church remain silent about such social sin? Our text forbids such silence. It condemns such social sin insofar as social sin nails Christ to the cross.

One more word on the subject (a word of freedom and responsibility) is proclaimed by our gospel story. It is interesting to note the kind of man who is released by the crowd's decision. It is Barabbas, a "notable [notorious] prisoner (Matthew 27:15)." Jesus' death set a criminal, a notorious sinner free!

Is this still not happening today? Is not Jesus' death still setting notable prisoners, sinners like us, free? Criminals challenge the social order. Might it not now be our task, as criminals set free by Christ's crucifixion, to challenge the social order and its institutions when they are working evil and harm to others? Our gospel for Passion Sunday calls the church to condemn sin when it permeates our social institutions. It also sets us sinners free (as Jesus' crucifixion set Barabbas free) to work for freedom and justice!

Palm Sunday
Matthew 21:1-11 (C, L)

God Works Through Opposites

God simply does not seem to do the sort of things we would expect our God to do. He does not always give us what we want. Most of us do not have everything we had hoped and dreamed for in life. He does not always answer our prayers. After all, we have all lost loved ones.

Sometimes God seems so far away. We pray to him, and nothing is there (or so it seems). We look to God to intervene in our world. Yet the hungry, the poor and the oppressed are still with us. Where is God? Why does he seem so powerless? What kind of a God do we really have? Have you ever asked these questions? I know that I have. And I suspect that you have, too.

What kind of a God do we really have? Our Bible lessons for today, in fact the entire theme of Palm Sunday, give us some insight into that question. They remind us that we have a God who works through contrasts (through opposites). Today on this Palm Sunday, we shall be talking a lot about the theology of the cross. We should do that every Sunday, but it is a special theme this week. God works through contrasts (through opposites).

There is an Old Testament scripture lesson that is very relevant at this point. In it, God comes right out and says this about himself. He says: "See now that I, even I, am he, and there is no god beside me; I kill and I make alive; I wound and I heal . . . (Deuteronomy 32:39)."

I kill, and I make alive. God, Yahweh, offers here an unambiguous testimony to the fact that he works through opposites. It is little wonder that God does not do the things we would expect a God to do. No wonder that he does not always give us what we want. No wonder that evil and oppression are still the order of the day, and that God still seems so powerless. It is all because we have a God who works through contrasts — who kills in order to make alive, who wounds in order to heal.

God's propensity to work through opposites — to use means which are entirely contrary to the ends which he aims to achieve — is apparent in today's second lesson from Philippians. In that text, Paul outlines how God revealed himself and his purposes through his Son. The eternal and divine Son of God, though in the form of God, "emptied himself, taking the form of a servant," and was born in the likeness of man (Philippians 2:6-7). Paul then proceeds to make another point about the Son: "And being found in human form he humbled himself and became obedient unto death, even death on a cross (Philippians 2:8)."

God works through lowly, ordinary things, through vehicles which are apparently contrary to his aims. The eternal, holy, omnipotent God becomes a lowly, ordinary man and even experiences the humiliation of death on a cross. Yet through such lowly means, God achieves just the opposite of lowliness. Christ is exalted! Thus Paul writes about the Son's death on a cross. Then he adds: "Therefore God has highly exalted him [Jesus Christ] and bestowed on him the name which is above every name, that at the name of Jesus every knee should bow, in heaven and on earth and under the earth, and every tongue confess that Jesus Christ is Lord, to the glory of God the Father (Philippians 2:9-11)." God works through contraries or opposing means in order to achieve his glorious aims.

We observe the same inclination in unambiguous clarity on Palm Sunday. In our gospel lesson we see the King, the Lord Jesus by whom God created the world, God himself comes to Jerusalem. The King; God himself! And he comes "humble, and mounted on an ass, and on a colt, the foal of an ass (Matthew 21:6; cf. John 12:15; Isaiah 62:11; Zechariah 9:9)." The glory of God on a humble ass. It is a study in contrasts. God always works through contrasts or opposites.

The crowd of disciples and followers of Jesus cheered him wildly on that first Palm Sunday. They treated him like a king. Fickle people. Just five days later they deserted him, and some may even have shouted, "Let him be crucified (Matthew 27:23)." God is always working through contrasts and opposites. We call this pattern in God's behavior the theology of the cross.

Of course, we know the final act in the drama. The crowd got its wish. The Jewish and Roman leaders put Jesus on that cross. And Jesus conquered! Jesus came back to life! His death made it possible for others who have died to come back to life (see 1 Corinthians 15:21ff). His death, his cross, give life! God is always working through contrasts or opposites.

It is on the cross that the contrasts are the most stunning. For on the cross we see God using death to give life. That is why the cross is the symbol of Christianity. That is why we call God's inclination to work through contrasts and opposites in order to achieve his aims, the theology of the cross.

What does it mean? What does all this imply for our Monday through Saturday lives? Palm Sunday and the theology of the cross explain the problems that I was talking about at the beginning of this sermon. They speak to the question of what kind of a God we really have. The theology of the cross (God's disposition to work through contrasts in order to achieve his aims) helps explain why God often seems so far away, so powerless, and sometimes seems irrelevant to us and to our needs. For God is a God who, because he works through contrasts and opposites, works in hidden ways. That is why he often seems so powerless and distant. It is because he is working in hidden ways, just like on the cross he gave us life in a hidden way.

Martin Luther often spoke of this aspect of the theology of the cross, concerning how God works in a hidden way through contrasts. In a series of lectures that Luther gave in 1515 and 1516 on the Book of Romans, he wrote: "For what is good for us is hidden, and that so deeply that it is hidden under its opposite. Thus our life is hidden under death, love for ourselves under hate for ourselves . . . salvation under damnation, heaven under hell . . . And universally our every assertion of anything good is hidden under the denial of it, so that faith may have its place in God, who is a negative essence and goodness and wisdom and righteousness, who cannot be touched except by the negation of all our affirmations."[1]

God can only be known through negations — through opposites. Why does he operate that way? Why does God operate in a hidden way by means of contrasts and negations? Martin Luther told us why in the quote that I just shared with you. God operates through contrasts and negations, he says, in order to exercise our faith.

How is our faith exercised by a God who works through contrasts and opposites? Martin Luther said it so well in one of his earliest sermons. He claimed that God works through contrasts (that God hides himself) in order to make us sinners.[2] He makes us sinners.

By making himself absent from us, by making it appear that he is powerless and unable to help us (unable to help our loved ones), God brings out our sin. His absence and his powerlessness lead us to doubt him and his goodness. In that way, by working under opposites, he shows us our sin. And we are sinners. We have doubted God's goodness and his existence in those moments when he seems so far away. (We are just like that fickle crowd of disciples on that first Palm Sunday.) This is one of the reasons that God works through contrasts and opposites. He is showing us our sin, so that we can be prepared to receive his message of forgiveness. As usual, the words of Luther are right on the money: "A true Christian [he says] must have no glory of his own and must to such an extent be stripped of everything he calls his own . . . Therefore we must in all things keep ourselves so humble as if we still had nothing of our own. We must wait for the naked mercy of God, who will reckon us just and wise."[3]

Remain humble as if you had nothing of your own. That is why God often hides himself. Luther says it beautifully again in one of his earliest sermons: "Therefore [he says] since he [God] can make just only those who are not just, he is compelled to perform an alien work in order to make them sinners before he performs his proper work of justification. Thus he says: 'I kill and I make alive; I wound and I heal.' "[4]

God hides himself. He does not seem to answer our prayers, he seems powerless, he kills, in order to show us our sin. Of course it is not that God wills the evil which befalls us. He does not want that to happen to us. It is simply the case that he does not deal with evil in quite the way that we would like him to do. I am talking about the times when he hides himself, does not seem to answer our prayers. In the doubts that we have about him, then, we see our sin more clearly.

Indeed, you and I really are like that fickle crowd of disciples on Palm Sunday. Yet we need such experiences. We need to see and to feel in our hearts that we have nothing to offer God. You need your false security, your false gods, destroyed. I do too. Only then are you truly ready to receive the forgiveness that Easter offers us. Only then are you ready to receive the salvation that God gives you.

The next time that you feel those doubts, the next time that you wonder about God, remember that God works through contrasts and opposites. He is using such doubts to show you your lack of faith — your sin. But take heart! For God kills in order to make alive. He is using your doubts to prepare you to receive him and his gift of salvation. That is the meaning of Palm Sunday. That is the meaning of your doubts and of my doubts. They show us our fickleness; they show us our lack of faith. They prepare us to hear God's life-giving gospel.

Martin Luther had one more observation about why God operates this way — under contrasts and opposites. In another of his sermons, he put it this way: "He [God] thrusts us into death and permits the devil to pounce on us. But it is not his purpose to devour us; he wants to test us, to purify us, and to manifest himself ever more to us, that we may recognize his love. Such trials and strife are to let us experience something that preaching alone is not able to do, namely, how powerful Christ is and how sincerely the Father loves us. So our trust in God and our knowledge of God will increase more and more, together with our praise and thanks for his mercy and blessing. Otherwise we would bumble along with our early, incipient faith. We would become indolent, unfruitful and inexperienced Christians, and would soon grow rusty."[5]

God works under opposites in order to help mature us in our faith so that we might appreciate even more the miracle of his love. And that love is truly miraculous.

Take heart when you suffer. Take heart, those of you who are suffering right now. Our God is a God who works under opposites, who kills in order to make (us) alive. He is working on you in your sufferings and anxieties that you might be feeling right now. He is working on you and me to give us new life and a fresh start!

Maundy Thursday
John 13:1-15 (C, RC)
John 13:1-17, 34 (L)

Wash Up First For The Meal Before You Eat!

"People just do not take the Lord's supper as seriously as they should. Perhaps it is the frequency with which we celebrate it. Too often we are merely going through the motions and not really getting out of it what we should. The problem is that we are not adequately prepared!"

Oftentimes I run across Christians who think this way and even explain their feelings. I am not advocating these sentiments if they are taken as an argument against frequent celebration of the sacrament. We can never receive too much love (too much of God's love)! However, a church committed to more frequent celebration of the Lord's supper needs to be on guard "lest familiarity breed contempt." We need to be prepared for the miracle that is about to enter our lives!

Another service of holy communion. It is nothing extraordinary, or so it seems. We have lived through many during the course of our lives. Are you excited about what is soon to transpire? If only we could share in the drama and excitement of that first Lord's supper! We are about to have that event recreated once again in our midst. If we tell the whole story and become immersed in the action that surrounds the meal, then I prophesy that our own celebration of the same meal may be a little more meaningful for you.

Here is the story: John's version of the Last Supper is a bit different from the accounts of the event which are offered by the other gospels. Not only is John's version distinct in his failure to provide many details about the actual meal (Jesus' words of institution). It is also distinct in the details he provides about Jesus' act of washing his disciples' feet at the meal. We need that kind of washing, too!

John's gospel tells us that during that final common meal between Jesus and his friends, Judas Iscariot resolved to betray Jesus (John 13:2). Of course, we already know that we have a God who works through contrasts — who brings good out of evil. Consequently, though it is surprising, it is very much in character that our Lord would bring good out of Judas' betrayal. Likewise, it is much in character that God would create good in the midst of Judas' evil at that first Lord's supper.

While Judas thought of ways to humiliate Jesus, our Lord himself, though fully aware of his own glory (John 13:3), undertook an act of self-humiliation. He washed his disciples' feet (John 13:5ff). It is one more indication of how much God loves his people. Even our treachery cannot quench his love!

Jesus washed the disciples' feet. Of course, in biblical times, washing your feet when you received hospitality from someone in their home was a standard custom. The guests had probably accumulated a good bit of dirt on their feet from the traveling that they had been doing. (Of course, sandals help accumulate more dust on your feet when you walk in them.) Usually in Old Testament times, the washing of feet was made possible by an invitation from the host, who often then offered guests the water and the guests washed their own feet (see Genesis 18:4; 19:2; 24:32; 2 Samuel 11:8). The washing was also a courtesy of the guest, an act by which guests cleansed themselves of the grime that they had accumulated in order truly to be worthy to enter and remain in the presence of their hosts.

Prior to Jesus, you washed your own feet when you were a guest. But Jesus took the next step in hospitality. He washed the disciples' feet for them!

Of course, Jesus' action, doing everything for his guests, is very much in character for God. He saves people that way; he does everything for them. He saves us through faith in Christ without any regard for works of the law that we might perform (Galatians 2:16). In the Old Testament practice of washing your own feet before socializing with your host, guests needed to do something to ready themselves for the fellowship that would follow with the hosts. But in the case of the Lord's supper, God did it all. The guest did not have to do anything. Fellowship with Jesus was not something that depended on a work of the disciples. They did not even have to wash their own feet before the meal. Jesus (God) did everything for them!

Peter did not want Jesus to wash his feet. Jesus told him later that he would understand the significance. But Peter still said "no" (John 13:7-8). Is that not the way it is with us? We are often too proud to want God to do everything for us. Or at least we are too proud to acknowledge that everything that we have is a gift from him. We do not accept gifts very well, do we? We inevitably seem to want to earn what we get. We like to think that God has been good to us, that he has given us what we have in life, because we deserve it. Yet that is not God's way. He gives his gifts free of charge.

The interaction between Jesus and Peter teaches us a number of lessons about how adequately to be prepared for the Lord's supper. You are not adequately prepared, it seems, unless you are willing to recognize that you are totally dependent on God's grace, that you have nothing to offer him. In short, you best prepare yourself for the sacrament by acknowledging how much you need it, because you have nothing you can offer to God.[1]

No, Peter and we do not at first want Jesus to wash our feet, to do everything for us. Peter's reluctance is just one more reminder of our sin. Yet the interaction Jesus had with Peter and us proceeds. That interaction gives us more clues concerning the kind of preparation that makes us truly ready to receive all the benefits that the Lord's supper provides.

First we cannot help but be struck by Jesus' humility in his act of washing his followers' feet. This was not a task that the host in Old Testament times undertook. You did it yourself, just like we today wash ourselves as we prepare for a meal or some other social event.

Even in the New Testament church, when Jesus' practice of washing the feet of Christian guests came to be adopted by his followers, it does not seem to have been much of a status job. The only reference we can find to the practice in the New Testament suggests that women did it (1 Timothy 5:10). Of course, in the largely sexist setting of New Testament times, if an activity was women's work, it was not worth much. Yet, our Lord, God himself, did that job on the evening of the last supper! God humbled himself by serving us, his followers.

Jesus makes it very clear in our Gospel lesson that he knew how humiliating a task he was undertaking. John writes: "When he [Jesus] had washed their feet, and taken his garments, and resumed his place, he said to them, 'Do you know what I have done to you? You call me Teacher and Lord; and you are right, for so I am. If I then, your Lord and Teacher, have washed your feet, you also ought to wash one another's feet. For I have given you an example [or pattern] that you also should do as I have done to you' (John 13:12-15)."

Later the story even continues, and John has Jesus say: "Truly, truly I say to you, a servant is not greater than his master; nor is he who is sent greater than he who sent him. If you know these things, blessed are you if you do them . . . . A new commandment I give to you, that you love one another; even as I have loved you, that you also love one another (John 13:16-17, 34)."

Jesus was aware that he had humbled himself, that he had assumed the role of a servant, when he washed the disciples' feet.[2] (Of course, the Bible gives testimony to the fact that servanthood is at the heart of Jesus' ministry; in his death he functioned as a servant who was humbled in executing the bidding of the Lord. He died serving us [Philippians 2:5-8; Isaiah 52:13—53:12; 49:1-6; 42:1-4].) Likewise, he seems to be calling us, his followers, to a similar life of servanthood. He wants us to live a life of servanthood — to love one another by serving each other.

An awareness of our total dependence on God along with this spirit of servanthood seem to be the kind of preparation for the Lord's supper that Jesus taught his disciples that evening of the very first sacramental meal. When you truly repent of all your pride and lean on our Lord, when you yearn to serve God and your neighbor, then you are adequately prepared for the sacrament. That is the sort of preparation that frees us truly to receive all the benefits that the Lord's supper provides — to experience the real significance of this sacrament in our lives! If you have truly repented of your pride, see yourself as totally dependent on God, yearn to serve him and your neighbor, then you will never again just go through the motions in receiving this sacrament. You will really be prepared to receive it.

Of course, there is still a problem with this whole matter of some kind of preparation for receiving the Lord's supper. It was Peter's problem. It is our problem, too.

Recall, that we and Peter were uneasy with Jesus' washing our feet. We want to do something about our salvation. We like to think or act as if we could make ourselves worthy to receive the sacrament and our salvation. But Jesus would not let him and us do the preparatory work. He did it for us!

It is good that God works that way. If we had to prepare ourselves to receive the Lord's supper and our salvation, we would never qualify. I am not truly repentant of my sins like I should be, are you? I am sometimes a bit uneasy with the idea that I cannot contribute to my salvation, are you not too? I would often rather exercise authority over others and be served, rather than to serve. How about you? Perhaps our failure on these points relates to why so often our faith and our reception of the sacraments is not a lively experience, but a mere "going through the motions."

If it were up to us to prepare ourselves to receive the Lord's supper we would be in big trouble. We would all fail the test.

This was Jesus' point in responding to Peter when he objected to having Jesus wash his feet. Jesus answered him and us, "If I do not wash you, you have no part in me (John 13:8)." Jesus needs to cleanse us from our sin, or we would have no part in him and in his Father's kingdom.

Peter finally saw the light. Eventually, God's Word gets through our thick skulls, through our pride, and we respond to God's call. "Lord, [do] not [wash] my feet only but also my hands and my head," Peter cried (John 13:9)." But Jesus' words point to the ultimate ingredient in an adequate preparation for receiving the Lord's supper. They seem to point us back to our baptisms.

Jesus is reported to have said to Peter, "He who has bathed does not need to wash, except for his feet, but he is clean all over; and you are clean (John 13:10)." We are clean! Our baptisms have made us clean; in your baptism your sins were washed away. That is how Paul talks about baptism (Ephesians 5:26; Titus 3:5).

A number of biblical scholars believe that, when John alludes to water in his gospel in connection with Christ, he is referring to Christian baptism.[3] Consequently, in the story of the last supper, John's and Jesus' allusion to washing is really a veiled reference to our baptisms. Baptism (or at least the benefits of Christ's death and resurrection as given by the Spirit) has already made us, the followers of Jesus, clean![4] Only our feet now need to be washed; in fact, however, our baptisms have made us clean all over (John 13:10a). The washing of our feet, which prepares the disciples and us for receiving the Lord's supper, is nothing more than a touch-up operation on merchandise that is already sound. Jesus' washing of the disciples' feet in order to prepare them and us for that last meal is nothing more than putting us all back in touch with who we already are — a kind of reminder of what our baptisms have already made us. Baptism is the one indispensable sign of our preparedness to receive the Lord's supper. We need to wash up first in the waters of our baptism before we eat the (communion) meal!

Of course, in one sense, this observation is so obvious that it seems rather trivial to devote a whole sermon to the theme. Since the time of the early church, being baptized has been a necessary prerequisite for admission to the Lord's supper.[5] You cannot receive the Lord's supper until you have been baptized.

However, there is something very profound about this realization. It is a word of gospel hope which frees us to receive the Lord's supper with confidence. The final word about being prepared for the Lord's supper is that ultimately we have all the preparation that we really need! We have been baptized! We already are clean!

John's version of the story of the last supper reminds us that we should be adequately prepared to receive the sacrament of holy communion if we want to obtain all its blessings to the fullest. It will mean a little more to you; this will not just be another communion service for you, if you come to the communion table aware of your total dependence on God, feeling repentant for your sins, and resolved to play the role of servant to our God and our fellow creatures.

Yet the good news is that this preparation work has already been done to you. Our preparation has been manifested. It happened to you in your baptism (Romans 6:1ff). We already have been made clean (Ephesians 5:26; Titus 3:5; John 13:10). The work of preparation, of repenting and resolving to live lives of servants, is nothing more than being what we already are. It is nothing more than an appropriation of our baptism. For a life lived denying your sin for the sake of God and your neighbor is the kind of person that your baptism made you. As such, it is not something we do. God has done it to us. He already has made us people who are sorry for our sin, aware of our total dependence on him, and ready to serve. That is the real you and me!

As you take a moment now to repent of your sin and stubbornness, to promise to live life anew as a servant to others, you are doing nothing more than becoming what you already are. It is sort of like the great natural athlete who engages in practice to sharpen his skills — to become what he already is. Jesus is just washing off the dust from our feet that beclouds this sort of cleanliness.

Come to the table, confident that God has already made you the kind of person who is ready to receive his sacrament. Come with the resolve to repent and to serve (because that is the kind of person God has already made you), and then his meal will be an occasion for deep spiritual enrichment — a true opportunity to wash off the dirt of sin from your otherwise clean body. You already have washed up, my friends; now come and eat the blessed meal that our Lord has brought for you and me and all his friends!

Good Friday
John 19:17-30

Why Did Jesus Have To Die?

"So they took Jesus, and he went out, bearing his own cross, to the place of a skull, which is called in Herbrew Gol'gatha. There they crucified him . . . (John 19:17-18)."

The story continues, and we know it well. He was crucified with two other criminals — one on each side. We know about the sign that Pilate hung on the cross — proclaiming Jesus (sarcastically) to be "King of the Jews (John 19:19-24)." We know about how the soldiers divided up his clothes (John 19:23-23). We ache when he thirsted, and they gave him vinegar (John 19:28-29).

Of course, there is that wonderful, moving moment when, though wracked by pain, he saw his mother and instructed the beloved disciple (probably John) to care for her (John 19:25-27). Even death could not overcome God's love. Death still cannot overcome his love!

Then it ended: "When Jesus had received the vinegar, he said, 'It is finished'; and he bowed his head and gave up his spirit (John 19:30)."

Unlike in the other gospel accounts, John's version of Jesus' crucifixion still portrays Jesus as being in control of things.[1] Yet the suffering was real and barbaric. Why? Why did he have to die? If God is all-powerful, and if Jesus truly remained in control of the situation as John seems to portray it, why did the Father not merely decree the forgiveness of our sins and leave it at that? Why did Jesus have to suffer and die for them?

In addition, even if Jesus did die for our sins, why is that so significant for Christians in the late 20th century? Is it not sufficient simply to proclaim God's love and his forgiveness? What is really at stake for the church and for us in getting clear about why Jesus had to suffer and die? These are not merely theological questions. They have implications for the way in which you live out your faith and relate to our Lord.

Why did Jesus have to die in order for our sins to be forgiven? For about 200 years or more the church has tended to dodge this question. The leading theologians and teachers of the church have tended not to deal with Christ's sacrificial death. It has been much easier to talk about the sacrificial lifestyle that Jesus lived for others, or merely to proclaim God's love and how Jesus reflects that love.[2] I, too, plead guilty of that retreat from attention to Christ's sacrifice.

Are we not all guilty of such indiscretion in our faith? If an ecumenical council were convened by the church in the next 10 years, and we threw out the idea that Christ's death was a necessary sacrificial offering for our sin, would your faith really be seriously affected? Would it not be sufficient for you simply to proclaim God's forgiving love? Be honest with yourself: What role is Christ's sacrificial death playing in your faith life?

There is a history of several hundred years behind this dilemma.[3] It has to do with a conflict between two of the most ancient views of the meaning of Christ's death. The one view dominated in the theology that began to prevail in Protestantism about 50 years after the reformation (Protestant Orthodoxy). Its roots were even more ancient, dating back at least to the theology that prevailed in the Middle Ages. This view of Christ's death taught that Jesus had to die in order to placate the wrath of God. God's justice or wrath has been offended by sin, and God demands punishment. Consequently,

Jesus must die in order to satisfy God's need to punish sin. (Especially see Ephesians 5:2; Hebrews 9:14).

What do you think of this way of understanding Christ's death? Given the influence of the schools of theology which espoused this view, it would not surprise me if many of you endorsed this idea of Christ's death as a satisfaction paid to God's wrath. However, such thinking has problems.

The main problem in thinking of Jesus' death in these terms is that it implies that salvation is not really God's work. Jesus is seen to be placating God. In a way, God is the enemy. That is not the kind of God whom we want or know. In addition, to understand Jesus' work on this day as a sacrifice paid to God seems to overlook some basic biblical themes. Among those that are overlooked are those portions of scripture that refer to Jesus' struggle with the devil and conceive of his death as a way of overcoming the devil's power. (Especially see Colossians 2:13-15.)

These alternative themes have been brought together by other Christian thinkers in a second, conflicting view of the atonement. On this view, Christ's death is regarded as having been necessary in order to trick the devil and defeat him by coming back to life. This second view makes sense in a number of respects. It makes sense to think of sin and evil as a power or force, which, like the devil, is more than our individual sins. Consequently, some of you may be attracted to this idea of Jesus' death as a consequence of God's struggle against the forces of evil.

This way of thinking about Jesus' death is also attractive for the picture of God it paints. It portrays God as more loving than the first explanation of Christ's death does. For while that first view in a sense made God the enemy (God's wrath must be satisfied if salvation is to be given), this second view of Christ's death as a consequence of the warfare with evil portrays God only as a God of love. God is not the enemy! He is fighting the enemy, sending Christ to destroy Satan.

Nevertheless, despite all of its strengths, this second approach to understanding Jesus' death has problems. Like the first view, it too has difficulties dealing with the whole range of the biblical witness. There are some passages of scripture which very clearly indicate the first understanding of Christ's death as a sacrifice paid by Christ to God. Ephesians 5:2 says it most clearly; it speaks of Christ as "a fragrant offering and sacrifice to God."

Consequently, we indeed have a kind of stand-off between the two prevailing views of the purpose of Christ's death. Neither is fully adequate. Little wonder that the church has been so relatively silent about the issue in the past few years. Little wonder that we do not tend to talk much about Christ's death and why he had to die. To limit ourselves merely to reflect on God's forgiving love seems to be the easy way out. Yet that route does not work either.

To neglect Christ's sacrificial death is to ignore the central symbol of the Christian faith — the cross. Such neglect makes grace cheap! To bypass the death of Christ, which confronts us so vividly today, cheapens grace because then we are ignoring the price that God paid to save us. In addition, if we ignore the price paid, we tend to ignore the depth or tragedy of our sin, and not take our sin as seriously as we should.

The church certainly has a knotty problem on its hands. However, our Good Friday story from the Gospel of John, and to some extent our second lesson (Hebrews 4:14-16; 5:7-9), may have a better way.[4]

The Jesus of John's gospel always has to be understood in the context of the famous prologue of the gospel (John 1:1-8). (In the second lesson, the author of Hebrews designates Jesus as both a "high priest [Hebrews 4:14-15]," who presumably offers a sacrifice through his death; yet the sacrifice presumably was not offered to a wrathful God since God is designated as the one who could save Jesus [Hebrews 5:7].) The prologue reminds the reader that Jesus is the eternal word of God through whom God created the world (John 1:1-3)." Everything that Jesus says or does in that gospel, even his death, must always be seen in the light of "the eternal will of God for the redemption of the world."[5] As the eternal Word who had a role in creation, all that Christ does is tied up with redeeming the world. Why did Christ have to die, according to John's scheme? In order to redeem the world.

In a sense, this point seems to offer us nothing that we did not previously recognize. Of course, Christ died to redeem the world. But why did the world require a death to redeem it? Once again we turn to John's prologue to the gospel. After introducing the Word, who is eternal and who created all things, John writes this: "In him was life, and the life was the light of men. The light shines in the darkness, and the darkness has not overcome it (John 1:4-5).''

And then John proceeds: "And from his [Christ's] fullness have we all received grace upon grace. For the law was given through Moses; grace and truth came through Jesus Christ (John 1:16-17)."

Christ's death must be understood in this context. His death was related to the struggle that God has with darkness, with sin and with chaos. Darkness, evil and chaos are all around us. You see them everywhere in the poverty, the anguish and the aimlessness that surround us. You experience them in your own heart, do you not? In his death this darkness sought to overcome Jesus, but it could not. Jesus died in the struggle with evil.

Yet, John also talks about Jesus' ministry, his death, as a means of grace in contrast to the law. Somehow, then, Jesus' death redeems the world by overcoming the demands of the law as well as by being part of a struggle with evil. How do we put these elements of a death that both overcomes the law as well as evil together? Our second lesson provides some clues. It speaks of Jesus as a "High Priest," who has presumably offered a sacrifice (Hebrews 4:14-15). To what or whom was the sacrifice offered? Later, in Hebrews (9:15-18), we are told that Christ is the mediator of a new covenant, "since a death has occurred which redeems them [us] from the transgressions under the first covenant . . . Hence the first covenant was not ratified without blood."

The point is quite apparent. Jesus' death, his sacrifice, was paid to the first covenant, to the law of God which he established with his people, first with Abraham and then on Sinai. This law (think of the ten commandments) is not just for Jewish and Christian people. The Bible tells us that God has written this law on human hearts; he has built it in to the very structures, the fiber, of creation (Romans 2:14-15). Consequently, by setting things right with the law (the commandments) by means of his death, Jesus was setting things right with creation. It is in this sense that John can speak of Jesus' work in redeeming the world.

The law, the commandments, by which the world is structured, had been violated by our sin. The law demands payment for such sin (see John 7:49; Romans 2:12; cf. Deuteronomy 6:3, 18; Psalms 89:31-32). This is why Jesus had to die; the law's just demands (that sinners must die for their sins) needed to be met. Why could God not merely abolish the law and wipe away the darkness of sin? Because the commandments were built into the very structures of creation, if he abolished the law, he would have to destroy us and the creation. Of course, God did not want to make that move. This is why Jesus had to die (to pay the law's commands), and God could not merely abolish the law and the darkness of evil.

The image here is of a world out of control. With sin in the world, God had a problem on his hands. He and his Son (the light) did not want to see his creatures eternally punished, as the law of his creation would dictate. Yet, because the world had been structured in this way, so that what is in violation of the law demands punishment, these demands of the law needed to be fulfilled or else the world's (legal) structure would have to be destroyed. John says the Word creates; the Word does not allow the darkness of evil and chaos to overcome its light (John 1:1-5). Consequently, God could not remedy the situation of darkness and evil by destroying the creation's structures. His only option, then, was to satisfy the law's demands by the sacrifice of his Son. This is what the cross is all about. This is why Jesus had to die.

In some sense, Jesus' sacrifice was paid to God, to his word of law in creation. (In this sense, this understanding of Christ's death embraces the biblical images which reinforce the first view of Christ's death that we noted.) However, the way that the law and creation were functioning was not what God wanted. In a sense they were God's enemy — out of control — had been co-opted by the darkness of evil and chaos. In order to overcome these enemies it was necessary for Jesus to suffer and die. (In this sense, this manner of talking about Christ's death also embraces the biblical images which reinforce the second viewpoint's idea that Christ's death was to overcome an enemy of God — in this case to overcome evil, chaos and a created order that had gotten out of control.)

What is at stake in all this for us and for our faith? Keeping in mind that the purpose of Christ's death was to set right the law of creation alerts us to the fact that Christ did not just die for you and me. If Christ's death was a sacrifice paid to the law, to the structures of the created order, then it follows that his death and God's redemptive work are on behalf of the whole of creation.

Christ's death and suffering, then, remind us that we are not saved alone. Salvation is not an individual affair. Christ's saving work on the cross was intended to straighten out the whole of creation. This entails that our Christian responsibility, as people who have been saved by the cross of Christ, also must include a concern for the whole of creation.

We need to keep Christ's sacrificial death before us in order to avoid a Christian individualism — to remind us that our salvation is linked with the redemption and restoration of the whole of God's creation. Christ died not just for you and me. He died to heal the whole of God's creation — the only way that he could deal with the darkness of sin without having to destroy his good creation in the process.

One more reason should be given for keeping Christ's death at the center of the faith. Our second lesson from Hebrews (4:15-16) says it well: "For we have not a high priest who is unable to sympathize with our weakness, but one who in every respect has been tempted as we are . . . Let us then with confidence draw near the throne of grace."

Christ's death reminds us of the kind of God whom we love. He is not a God "out there," untouched by human suffering. He is a God who is Jesus Christ, and who as Jesus Christ has suffered. We see him suffering in our gospel lesson when he thirsted on that cross (John 19:28) and when he gave it all up and said, "It is finished (John 19:30)." Yes, we have a God who knows our despair, our trials — an emphathetic God who has experienced our suffering.

What is at stake in keeping Christ's death at the center of our faith? Nothing less than a full appreciation of the extent of God's redeeming love — a reminder that that love is for all creation and is given by a God who has empathized and suffered with us. Praise God that he is a God like that — a God who suffered and died for us and for his whole creation. His cross has wrought so much good. It really is a Good Friday!

The Resurrection Of Our Lord
John 20:1-18 (C, L)
John 20:1-9 (RC)

The Empty Tomb

"Now on the first day of the week Mary Magdalene came to the tomb early, while it was still dark, and saw that the stone had been taken away from the tomb. So she ran, and went to Simon Peter and the other disciple, the one whom Jesus loved, and said to them, 'They have taken the Lord out of the tomb, and we do not know where they have laid him.' Peter than came out with the other disciple, and they ran toward the tomb (John 20:1-3). Then Simon Peter came . . . and went into the tomb; he saw the linen cloths lying (John 20:6). Then the other disciple who reached the tomb first, also went in and he saw and believed; for as yet they did not know the scripture, that he must rise from the dead. Then the disciples went back to their homes (John 20:8-10)."

The story continues: "But Mary stood weeping outside the tomb, and as she wept she stooped to look into the tomb; and she saw two angels in white, sitting where the body of Jesus had lain, one at the head and one at the feet. They said to her, 'Woman, why are you weeping?' She said to them, 'Because they have taken away my Lord, and I do not know where they have laid him.' Saying this, she turned round and saw Jesus standing . . . (John 20:11-14a)."

John proceeds to tell the story of how at first Mary did not recognize the Risen Christ. Eventually, when he called her by name, she recognized him! Next, Jesus instructs her to tell his followers that he would be ascending into heaven (John 20:14b-17). John then proceeds to tell us the rest of the story: "Mary Magdalene went and said to the disciples, 'I have seen the Lord'; and she told them that he had said these things to her (John 20:18)."

How fitting it is that on this great festival of Easter, the Bible readings assigned by the church should be so powerful as they are today. Take off your shoes, people; you are on holy ground (see Exodus 3:5; Joshua 5:15). Today's texts capture that holy moment when the biblical witness and the realities of our ordinary lives intersect. You and I are on holy ground! Believe it! Your life, your everyday life, and our Bible reading from John about the resurrection are meshing together.

Mary Magdalene, Peter, and the beloved disciple (probably John), did not really understand what was transpiring when they saw the empty tomb. Of course, John says that the beloved disciple believed when he saw the empty tomb. Yet it did not seem really to have much of an impact on him at first. John reports that he and Peter saw the empty tomb and just went home. (They did not seem to comprehend that Jesus had risen, or at least they did not appreciate its significance.) They had beheld a miracle. And all John can say about it is that they went home.

It took an actual appearance by Jesus to Mary, to really set things straight. (Prior to her actually seeing the Risen Jesus, she had been scared and upset.) Only when the disciples had word of the Risen Lord or saw him themselves did they believe and were ready to take up his ministry of the new life he had given them.

Why was there so much initial confusion and lack of understanding among Jesus' followers until they actually met the Risen Lord? The failure of Mary and the disciples to get things right has something to do with our own failure to take the joyful message of Easter to heart and to live that way every day of our lives.

Easter Sunday. What a glorious day it is! For many of us, our loved ones are with us. The church is filled. Everybody feels happy, or even if we miss a loved one, at least we have some peace of mind. God seems so real today. The resurrection of our Lord seems so real. We could hardly doubt it.

Where will these feelings be next week? Where will they be tomorrow? I can tell you where these feelings and our Easter spirit will be next week. They will be gone! The joy and the peace we feel on this glorious Easter will be gone (or at least it will not be as much in evidence as it is today). The church will not be filled, as it is today. I hope that I am wrong, but I prophesy it.

Those of us who will be here next Sunday will not feel as good about worship as we do today. We probably will not feel today's joy and peace with quite the same intensity. We will not be quite as certain about God and about our Lord's resurrection — at least some of us may not be. In fact, further down the road, months ahead, perhaps there will be times when the events of life or what we read lead us to doubt God and his goodness — to make us wonder about the truth of the story about our Lord's resurrection.

Consequently, we will share with the disciples and Mary their initial confusion, lack of understanding, and apathy. Those of you who do not plan to be here next Sunday are already walking down the disciples' path. You and I really cannot believe that the tomb is empty, and, if we do, we are not inclined to do anything about it, but merely observe the data and return to our homes untouched by it all. Why? Why are we so often inclined to react to the Easter story in that way?

In order to unpack these questions I need to give you all a brief lesson in historical-critical biblical studies (the study of the Bible the way biblical scholars do it). The doubts, uncertainty, or lethargy that we and the disciples feel has something to do with the character of the resurrection accounts and the fact that too often we only have half the story about Jesus' resurrection.

Most biblical scholars teach that the gospels' and the epistles' accounts of the first Easter include two distinct, originally independent traditions of stories about the resurrection.[1] (Remember, the New Testament, especially the gospels, were not eyewitness accounts but were based on stories about Jesus' life that were told among the first Christians.) Of course, you have the stories of Jesus' appearances after the resurrection. (Let us call them the "appearance tradition.") In the account of the first Easter by John that we have been considering, we do not encounter this tradition of stories until Mary actually meets the Risen Christ after Peter and the beloved disciples have gone to their homes.

Side-by-side these stories of the resurrection appearances you have another tradition of stories about the resurrection. These stories say nothing about actually seeing the Risen Lord Jesus. They merely report the fact that his tomb was empty. We call this second set of stories the empty tomb tradition. Our gospel lesson for today from John employs this empty tomb tradition (all the way to the point where Peter and the beloved disciple return to their homes [John 20:10]).

The other tradition of stories (the appearance tradition) is especially evident in our second lesson from 1 Corinthians. It is also evident in the gospels of Matthew (28:9-10, 16) and Luke (24:13-53). (Also see the longer ending of Mark [16:9-20].)

At any rate, my purpose in providing you with this information about the two traditions of resurrection stories is to explain to you more clearly why Jesus' followers originally reacted to the empty tomb with misunderstanding, confusion, sadness (in the case of Mary), or apathy. This will also shed some light on why we do not always believe and act on the testimony of scripture's witness to the resurrection as we should.

We need to note a recurring pattern in the stories about the empty tomb (the tradition which John borrowed in his account of the resurrection up to the point that Peter and the beloved disciple returned to their homes [John 20:10]). In all of the gospels, wherever the empty tomb tradition is employed, disbelief, confusion or apathy make themselves evident among the followers of Jesus (John 20:1-11; Luke 24:1-11; Matthew 28:1-4; Mark 16:1-8). We think of Thomas and the doubts that he had when he only heard the stories of Jesus' resurrection. He needed to see the Risen Lord himself before he could really be excited in his faith (John 20:24-29).

When the story of the empty tomb is proclaimed, the usual reaction is disbelief, confusion or apathy. In some cases, the hearers decide to keep the news as a secret (Mark 16:8; cf. John 20:10). Or, as in our gospel lesson for today, Jesus' followers fail to understand (John 20:9), react apathetically (John 20:10), or despair (John 20:11). It is only when Jesus' followers experience the Risen Lord, only in the appearance tradition stories, is the certainty of belief in the resurrection (without fear) assured (John 20:16ff; Matthew 28:9-10; Luke 24:13ff). That is the way the Bible reads.

Do you see the point? That is why Peter, the beloved disciple, and Mary Magdalene did not at first react to the empty tomb with joy, enthusiasm and understanding. They had not yet actually experienced the Risen Lord!

This is our problem with the gospel of Jesus Christ today. Too many of us only meet the Risen Lord once or twice per year. All we know (existentially and experientially) is the story of the empty tomb.

Where is he? Where can we meet the Risen Lord? He is here every Sunday. Anytime two or three gather in his name, he has promised to be present (Matthew 18:20). You can meet him here in church every Sunday. If you pray at home or on the road, read your Bible with a few others, you will probably meet him, too, on these occasions. In fact, the next time we celebrate the Lord's supper (as we are today), I guarantee that you will meet the Risen Lord. He comes to us in the bread and wine. He has promised it (1 Corinthians 11:23-26; Mark 14:22-24; Matthew 26:26-28; Luke 22:19-20)! That is why we are all so joyful, all so confident in our faith today. It is because we are all in the presence of the Risen Christ. He is here with us right now!

Consequently, if doubts about Jesus' resurrection, if doubts about God, come your way, or if you are feeling apathetic and not excited about Christian faith today or tomorrow, then chances are that you are a bit like Mary Magdalene, Peter, and that other disciple on that first Easter. Chances are, you have only been hearing the stories about the resurrection. You have not actually been in the presence of the Risen Lord enough. Or if you do worship regularly, but still feel the doubts, the uncertainties, and the lack of enthusiasm that I have been describing, then you have not been paying enough attention to your meetings with the Risen Lord. Perhaps you have not had the right mental attitude for worship.

Let me tell you: When you live in the presence of Jesus, every Sunday, when you do not just attend, but hang on every word, when you commune regularly, pray at home daily, read your Bible, involve yourself in the study of the Bible, get active in church programs — when you live with Jesus every day, then your doubts, confusion and apathy cannot help but begin to take care of themselves. Then you will realize that you possess all the evidence you will ever need to convince you of the truth of the resurrection! Then you will be sure that God exists. You will see him everywhere. Then your faith will truly matter to you!

God has provided (he is still doing) enough to convince us all of the truth of Christianity and of his Son's resurrection — enough to get you excited about your faith. It is merely a matter of living with the Risen Lord, a matter of living with Jesus. He is here every Sunday; he is present in your Bible. It is merely a matter of coming here, of listening, of reading, of praying and of serving.

He is risen! Believe it! He is present among us; just come, and open your eyes. Christ is risen! All that is destructive and painful in your life is dead. In every facet of your life you have been given a fresh start with Christ (Colossians 3:3-4). Christ is risen indeed!

Mark Ellingsen — Easter 2-A
Preparation and Manifestation

Easter 2
John 20:19-31

What Happens When We Can't Believe It?

All three of our Bible lessons for today touch on themes that cannot help but direct our attention to last Sunday's celebration of the festival of Easter. (The Roman Catholic lectionary's first lesson [Acts 2:42-47] reminds us of the Easter festival, as its reference to the community shared among the early Christians is reminiscent of an active church member's joy in seeing a packed church on Easter Sunday.) I do not know about your feelings with certainty, but I suspect that last Sunday's worship service (what with it being Easter and with the church packed with our whole church family) felt as good to you as it did to me. It was a real spiritual high. For what was happening last Sunday, what with everybody happy and enjoying each other, was a lot like what was happening for the very first Christians when they actually encountered the Risen Lord (John 20:18; Luke 20:52-53; Mark 16:20; Matthew 28:9).

I know that is the way I felt last Sunday. With all of my brothers and sisters worshiping, not just because it was Easter and the thing to do, but here because you all believe in Jesus Christ, the experience made God a little more real for me. It was clear that I am not the only one who believes in Jesus' resurrection and in God's love. Obviously you and all your fellow worshipers believe in him, too! That realization felt so good to me. God and the resurrection really seemed a little more real. And when you feel that way it truly is a spiritual high.

However, what happens to you when you are not on that kind of spiritual high? What happens when God does not seem quite as real — those times when life has got you down in the dumps and you just do not feel its joy? Perhaps some of you are feeling kind of low like that right now and do not feel the joy about which I was speaking.

Of course, if you do not feel this kind of joy, if God's love does not seem to be getting through to you today, if it is all just so many words, do not hang your head in shame. Do not do that, because my time is coming, too — my time and everybody else's who is feeling good. Our time is coming, too — our time when life will not be quite as joyful and when God will not seem very real. Yes, our time is coming, too; there is no escaping spiritual death.

Spiritual death. Several times during Lent we talked about spiritual death — the feeling that we are just going through the motions, that life does not have much purpose, the feeling that God is not doing what we need from him. I am talking about those times when life is getting you down or when you are not sure you believe. All of us have had these feelings. Have you not, too?

All of our Bible lessons for today have something to say about the problem of spiritual death and the struggle to believe. We start with the gospel and our second lesson. First, in our second lesson from the first letter of Peter (2:19-25), you have Peter writing to Christians who, to put it frankly, were going through a living hell. Life was really treating them rotten, sort of like it does for us sometimes (1 Peter 1:6; 3:13-14, 16-17; 4:12; 5:10). And in the middle of all the suffering being inflicted upon them it was only natural that the people to whom Peter wrote would start to wonder why. Why? Why would a loving God put me through all that? I do not feel his love; life is too rough for that. (See 1 Peter 2:7-8.)

Does it sound familiar? Do such feelings and doubts hit home? They sure do for me. In my own life, you see, I know that the times when I feel the most distant from God are the times when I do not feel good about life or myself. I cannot feel God's love on those occasions, and so it is sort of difficult to believe in him. I cannot see what he is doing in my life, cannot see how he is helping me, and so on those occasions I do not feel like helping him and his church. My prayer life suffers, and I start to feel spiritually dead. Christianity is not very important to me then. I just do not feel like it, and the investment I would need to put in it.

"Prove it to me, God! Prove it to me." That is what I am really saying in those moments of apathy and hopelessness. "Make my life good; give me peace, then I will believe and love you, God." Does it sound familiar? Do you hear a little bit of yourself in my confession of sin?

We all sound a lot like "doubting Thomas" in our gospel lesson for today. "Unless I see in his hands the print of the nails, and place my finger in the mark of the nails . . . I will not believe (John 20:25)." That is what Thomas said, when he had missed sharing the experience the other disciples had had with the Risen Lord. "Until I feel your love, God, until you give me joy and make life good, until then, God, I do not want too much to do with you."

That is our version of Thomas' doubts. However, we do not have Thomas' "guts." We do not usually bring our doubts and questions directly to God and our fellow Christians like Thomas did (John 20:25). (Thomas, you see, was very much the disciple with a questioning faith; he was the kind of believer whose faith was enriched by asking questions. We know that from other stories in John's gospel [14:5]. Thomas had a lively, questing faith [John 11:16].) No, we are more subtly dishonest in hiding the weaknesses in our faith. We tend to "cop-out," to avoid involvement, to become slack in prayer and worship, because after all, we do not feel any better after engaging in such activities. I just do not feel it any more. I feel spiritually dead, so why bother?

All of us have times in our life when we feel this way, right? I refer to those times when it is just not happening between you and God, when life is not very sweet or at least not that beautiful. Of course, we do.

Have you noticed where the problem lies? There is a pattern to our spiritual malaise. The problem is that we are spending too much time, like Thomas (and perhaps like the Christians to whom Peter wrote), being hung up on our feelings. Thomas did not feel that Jesus could possibly rise from the dead; consequently he did not believe what the other disciples told him.

The Christians to whom Peter was writing could not feel God's love, what with all the torture that they were enduring. Too many times we do not feel like worshiping God or loving other people, and so we do not. We really are too hung-up on our own feelings, on ourselves, for our own (and our neighbors') good.

How about it, folks? This train of thought makes a lot of sense to me. I know that when it comes to being happy in life, when it is a matter of my relationship with God, a lot of times I am my own worst enemy. I am too hung-up on myself and how I feel, and I need to get away from myself. That is how it was with "doubting" Thomas and for the Christians to whom Peter was writing. They needed to get away from themselves and their feelings. We learn a lot about ourselves and our way of behaving from them.

How do we get out of this mess? How can we awake from spiritual death? How can we find joy in life? How can we get a fresh start? All three (or two) of our assigned Bible lessons today give us a simple answer: Believe in the Risen Lord. Hang on, forget your feelings, and have faith in Jesus Christ (John 20:26-29; 1 Peter 1:3-7; Acts 2:22-24, 31-32).

How can I do it? How can I believe in Jesus' resurrection and in God's love for me? How can I believe it when I do not feel his love or when I do not feel any joy in life?

Martin Luther once tried to answer these questions, and what he said makes a lot of sense to me. It is what our Bible lessons are all trying to say. At any rate, Luther's point was that sometimes "feeling is against faith and faith is against feeling." Here is exactly how he put it one time in one of his Easter sermons: "To this I reply: I have often said before that feeling and faith are two different things. It is the nature of faith not to feel, to lay aside reason and close the eyes, to submit absolutely to the Word, and follow it in life and death. Feeling however does not extend beyond that which may be apprehended by reason and the senses, which may be heard, seen, felt and known by the outward senses. For this cause feeling is opposed to faith and faith is opposed to feeling."[1]

Feeling is against faith, and faith is against feeling. Sometimes I do not feel loved; sometimes I do not feel joy; sometimes life seems pretty meaningless and my faith feels empty; but the resurrection faith proclaims that I am loved, that life is full of meaning! Our faith is certain, Martin Luther once said, because "it snatches us away from ourselves and places us outside ourselves." We do not depend on ourselves, but are snatched away from ourselves and our fears. We do not have to depend on ourselves, our own strength, and our own experience. We do not have to depend on ourselves because we are dependent on something outside of ourselves, that is, dependent on the promises of God.[2]

This is what Peter is telling us in our second lesson. This is what Jesus is telling Thomas and us in our gospel lesson. "People," they are saying, "don't get so hung-up on yourselves that you forget God's love. Perhaps you do not feel that love right now, but that does not mean that he is not loving you. Perhaps it does not feel like he is making much of a difference in your life, but that does not mean that he is not. He is giving you joy, even when you do not feel it."

Our gospel lesson (and the second lesson) tells us, "look people, sometimes you have to believe against the way you feel." Especially this is Jesus' point to Thomas, when he calls Thomas and us to faith even though we do not directly feel (or experience) his resurrection (John 21:29; cf. 1 Peter 1:6-8). It is not what you feel that counts; it is what God does and says that counts.

Of course, this is not the whole story. Our Bible lessons for today make another point. Praise the Lord for it! For if the only way to be raised out of our spiritual doldrums were to depend on your own personal faith, then we would all be in trouble. None of us as individuals has that strong of a faith. But together we do!

These reflections bring us back to the beginning of this sermon and to those good feelings I had when I worshiped with all of you last week. It brings me back to that feeling of closeness that I had to God last Sunday, because I knew that all of you and our absent friends, not just me, but all of you believe in him, too!

All three of the Bible lessons are proclaiming this message. All of them testify to the way in which our faith is strengthened by each other. It is no accident that Thomas came to believe in the resurrection when he was in the company of all the rest of the disciples (John 21:26-29). Jesus is usually most present and reveals himself when his people are assembled in community. And it is no accident that Thomas' doubts about the resurrection were initiated because he was not sharing in fellowship with the other disciples (but was off by himself) the first time that Jesus appeared to them (John 20:24-25).

The same Word is indirectly proclaimed in our second lesson (1 Peter 1:3-9). By themselves, the Christians to whom Peter was writing may have been floundering in their sufferings. But Peter and his cohorts reached out to comfort them. These Christians of Asia Minor to whom Peter wrote were comforted and strengthened by their brothers and sisters in Christ.

The message is also delivered in our first lesson. Peter is preaching on the first day of Pentecost to various Jews in Jerusalem. He proclaims Christ's resurrection (Acts 2:14ff). He delivers his sermon flanked by all of the other disciples (no doubt for support; see Acts 2:14). Then he even concludes his testimony to the resurrection by noting that all of his fellow believers make the same testimony (Acts 2:32). Peter is clearly gaining strength and courage from the fact that he shares a common faith with the other disciples. (Note for those using the Roman Catholic lectionary's first lesson [Acts 2:42-47]. This lesson recounts how the followers of Jesus, just after his ascension and Pentecost, shared everything. The following observations about the text could be made: In the very first church, the early Christians shared everything; they did everything together; they leaned on each other.)

This kind of sharing, this kind of leaning on each other, is the purpose of the church. It is why God created the church — so that we Christians could lean on each other when the going gets rough, and when it is hard to believe in a loving God (1 Corinthians 12:24b-26).

Perhaps I do not feel joy, excitement, love and enthusiasm about the faith. Yet when I am down, if I can lean on some of you, on some of you who are feeling joy in life, feeling loved by God, and excited about it, then it is just a bit easier for me to fight my feelings of apathy, sadness and my weak faith. Being with people who are excited, feel God's love, and are happy about it, makes God a lot more real. Some of those good feelings are liable to rub off on the rest of us. Oh, of course, when the rest of you need it, and we weak ones are stronger, then you can lean on us.[3]

My friends, this is the purpose of the church. This is what worship, congregational service projects, church meetings and fellowship events are all about. They aim to facilitate our sharing and leaning on each other. They aim to get us so enmeshed in God's love and the Easter joy that goes with it (to make us experience the new life that Christ has given us), that pretty soon we forget our feelings — so that without even recognizing it we begin to feel good. All of our Bible lessons for today are pointing us to what is happening right now among us — to the church. The cure for unhappiness and for spiritual death is right here, on mornings like this and in service projects like our congregation conducts. It is all here waiting for us to participate.

It is indeed God's gift to me that you really believe in him, too. It makes believing in him and his love a little easier for all of us. Praise God that the new life that he has given us at Easter and in our baptisms includes all of us (all the faithful) together! Such an insight about our common faith makes me feel good after all. Thank God that he has given us each other!

Easter 3
Luke 24:13-35

What Happens To You When You Die?

"What happens to you when you die, Dad?" "Of course, son, if you believe in God, you go up to heaven where you will be with God and the angels."

Does such a response sound familiar to you? Is not this the answer with which most of us were raised: That when you die, your soul, free from the body, will go to heaven. Is that what happens? Is that what you all think? Do not despair. I shall not call for a show of hands, but I do want you to think about your answer to the question of what we will be like after we have died (in faith). "And I believe in the resurrection of the body, and the life everlasting. Amen."

The resurrection of the body. Week after week you and I recite the creed. We say that we and all Christians believe in a resurrection of the body. We are not proclaiming the idea of a soul floating up there somewhere in heaven. Rather, we proclaim a resurrection of our bodies. Christians, what happens to you when you die? We believe in the resurrection of the body.

In the modern church we have not been too inclined to grapple with questions concerning some end time in the future (future eschatology). For me, it has always seemed sufficient to concern ourselves with our relationship with God right now.

The supposition is that if you know that God truly loves you, then eternal life will take care of itself.

However, lately it has become apparent to me, what with the media's attention to exotic forms of spirituality, to cults, to devil worship, that many of our brothers and sisters in Christ are struggling with the question of what happens to the faithful when they die. Then Easter came. Of course, Easter has an answer to our question; what it is all about is eternal life. This week, as I planned the sermon, this range of issues especially drew my attention. It struck me that in this morning's gospel lesson we have the real answer to our questions: What happens to you when you die, and what is the resurrection of the body?

Perhaps in your thinking about the gospel story of Jesus' resurrection appearance to two of his followers on the road to Emmaus, you are prepared to challenge me: "Come on, Pastor, that gospel lesson does not have anything to do with our resurrection. It has to do with Jesus' resurrection and the difficulties that those two followers had in recognizing him. It is a nice story. But what does it have to do with the way things will be for us after we die?"

Patience, friends. What happened to Jesus, what he did, and what he looked like after he rose from the dead have everything to do with the way that things will be for you and me after we die.

How do I know that the Risen Lord is the paradigm for our resurrection? Paul told me. Here is what he said: "But in fact Christ has been raised from the dead, the first fruits of those who have fallen asleep (1 Corinthians 15:20)."

Did you hear that? Jesus' resurrection from the dead on Easter is our guarantee that all of us who believe in him will have a resurrection like his. Hear the words of Paul once more: "For if we have been united with him (with Christ in our baptisms — that is what happens in baptism, folks, we die with Christ) in a death like his, we shall certainly be united with him in a resurrection like his (Romans 6:5)." We shall be united with Christ in a resurrection like his resurrection.

The biblical witness is about as clear as it can get at this point. If you want to find out what happens after you die, in one sense, Christians really do not know. The Bible does not say much about what will happen to us after we die until Jesus comes again. (Sometimes it suggests that the dead go right to heaven to be with God [Revelation 7:9-14; Luke 16:22-31]. Sometimes it suggests that the dead merely sleep [1 Corinthians 15:20, 51; 1 Thessalonians 4:14].) When Christ does come, however, we know that there will be a resurrection — that we will be raised to life pretty much in the same way that Jesus was raised on the first Easter (1 Corinthians 15:22-23; 1 Thessalonians 4:13-17; Romans 6:5). Consequently, if you want to know what it will be like for us when we, who have died believing in Jesus, are raised from the dead, then we find our clues by paying attention to what Jesus was like after he had risen from the dead. That is what life will be like for us when we are raised.

What was Jesus like? Today's gospel lesson gives us some clues. First of all, we know that Jesus had a body, and he was walking right here on earth (Luke 24:15ff; cf. Philippians 3:21; John 20:27; Luke 24:39-40). No, he was not just a soul floating around in the clouds. He had a body! That is why we Christians do not just confess our faith in a heaven for souls, but in a resurrection of the body — of our bodies. Eternal life with God is always life with a body.

Indeed, Jesus still had his body after the resurrection. Yet it must have been a little different from his body before he died. After all, the two men whom Jesus met that day on the road to Emmaus had been followers of Jesus. They had known him (Luke 24:13-14). Yet for some reason they did not at first recognize Jesus when he joined them on that road (Luke 24:16). There must have been something different about him.

Of course, Jesus had not completely changed; he was basically the same person that he had always been. And finally these two followers were able to recognize him; they recognized him when they all sat down to eat (Luke 24:29-31a).[1] But once they had recognized him, Jesus vanished before their very eyes (Luke 24:31b).

The events indicate Jesus was different. After his resurrection, nothing could stop him. He was no longer locked in by the boundaries of space and time. I imagine that there was a kind of glow of radiance, a glow of happiness, all around him (sort of like the way he looked when the transfiguration occurred [Luke 9:29; Matthew 17:2]). Perhaps that is why the two men never recognized him until they were eating that meal together.

Friends, this morning's gospel lesson truly provides us with some clues concerning what our resurrected bodies will be like. When we look at Jesus after his resurrection we know that we shall still have our bodies when we rise from the dead. Basically, they will still be the same. I shall look like me (though perhaps a little better, I hope)! But I shall still be me and you will still be you. We shall be the same. However, just like Jesus, we shall not be "locked in" by anything, not even by our old hang-ups. At the resurrection, I shall be a perfect me — able to do everything I always liked to do and could do, only I shall be able to do them better.

Paul has a beautiful way of talking about the meaning of death and what God will do about it. He says it in the 15th chapter of his first letter to the Corinthians.

Here is what Paul says. He says that at the final resurrection, our bodies will be like beautiful plants that spring from grungy seeds (1 Corinthians 15:35ff). Of course, a beautiful potato, for example, needs to have a seed or it will never grow. But once it grows, where is the seed? To be sure, it came from a seed. But the seed is not there anymore; in a sense the seed died.

Paul suggests that our lives are a little like these seeds. The bodies that you and I have, the lives that we are living, are a bit like the seeds that God is planting. Someday a beautiful plant will grow from that seed. That beautiful plant which will stem from you is your resurrection body, the perfect you — the way God originally intended you to be.

Of course, for all that to happen, in order for your resurrection body to grow, the seed has to disappear. It has to die.

That is why even though Jesus died for our sins, we still have to die. We die, so that those beautiful plants, the perfect you and me, can blossom in the sunlight of God's love. The perfect you and me, without our hang-ups and short-comings, the way we would have been if we had not sinned, this is what we have to look forward to after we die — when Jesus comes again. That stranger on the road to Emmaus demonstrated to those two followers of his what our resurrected bodies would be like.

I do not know about you folks, but there is something so wonderfully inviting in these images. In eternal life I am going to be me — to have a body like this one, to be able to do the things that I do well — only better. Yes, that certainly beats playing a harp and flying all around heaven. I hate harps!

For my money, the Christian vision of the resurrected life also beats getting swallowed up by everything else in the unity of our oneness (as is implied by the religions of Asia).[2] No, you can have it, because I like being me. And God proclaims that even in death I shall still be me — only better!

There is something beautiful in the Christian image of the resurrection life; it is almost majestic in its beauty. The message of Jesus on the cross is that God loves us just the way we are! He loves us so much that he wants us to be ourselves forever.

When you think about the resurrection life this way, the words that Paul once wrote really make sense; they are the final word that needs to be spoken about death and resurrection: "O death, where is thy victory? O death, where is thy sting (1 Corinthians 15:5)?"

Easter 4
John 10:1-10
Led By The Shepherd

Decisions, decisions. Life is full of decisions. In fact, a number of philosophers and psychologists tell us that the decisions we make (or our behavior) largely make us who we are.[1] Life is nothing but decisions. How do we make them in a Christian manner? We Christians believe that by his resurrection on Easter, Christ has given us new life (1 Peter 1:3). You have been given a new life! Now that we have that new life, how does it affect the way in which we make decisions? At least two of our Bible lessons and our psalm this Sunday of the Good Shepherd give us some idea of an answer to these questions.

In observing how I and other people make decisions, I have noticed a pattern in the way we proceed. When the going gets tough, when a Christian decision has to be made, we tend to fall back into our old comfortable ways of doing things. We start relying on our instincts. How about it, friends? Is that not how you and I usually make our decisions?

Some of us have the instincts of a businessman (or woman). When it comes time to make a decision, the first thing we think about is growth and profit. How can we earn or save money? How can we keep our "nest egg?" Yes, that is what we need to do.

Others of us have the instincts of a reformer. The status quo must be challenged. The system is not working. Whatever promotes freedom and liberation from opresive existing structures is good, and we must get behind such movements. Live for today; let the future take care of itself. The great enemy is continuity and the boredom it produces.

Still others of us have the instincts of a conservative: We have always done it that way here at church and here in our community. So why change the system? A few proponents of that attitude can be found in this parish; what do you think?

Finally, we have the pragmatists or politicians. We should do whatever it takes to keep everybody happy. We do not want to rock the boat. (I do not want to decide anything that will hurt my good name, and what I do decide must be in the interest of my retaining control.) Hm, such attitudes are not unfamiliar to any of us.

Have you found a little of yourself in one or more of these attitudes? If you are honest with yourself, you probably did; I know that there is something of me in these types of decision-making. All of the types have something to do with me (and you), because all of those ways of making decisions have something in common. Behind them all is the "gut-feeling" upon which all of us rely when we make a decision. (This "gut-feeling" is a symptom of our sin.) It is the "Do your own thing" gut-feeling. I am doing what I do, I am deciding this way, because that is the way I like it. I do not like it that other way.

Have you ever caught yourself saying or thinking such things? I know that I have to plead guilty. It would hardly be surprising, since a number of social analysts have observed how American, if not all Western society in the waning decades of our century, has been characterized by the emergence of particular value-systems authorized by nothing more than our mad quest for individual self-fulfillment.[2] Our participation in such a cultural ethos raises hard questions for us: To the degree that our decisions are made with reference to our personal preference, are any of us really making Christian decisions in the way we are living our lives? Are we just throwing our faith aside most of the time, even if we are here Sunday mornings? Have we lost our way? Have we been throwing away the "abundant life" that Jesus promises us in our gospel lesson (John 10:10b)? How can we get it back?

Take heart, friends! Our sin and our selfishness have not lost us the new life that Jesus gave us in his resurrection and in our baptisms. "The gifts and the call of God are irrevocable (Romans 11:29)." Even when we are enemies of God, he loves us and wants to save us (Romans 5:10). However, we have not been making use of the gift that God has given us. Perhaps the gift of the abundant life has not been informing us in the way we are living — in the way in which we make our decisions.

It is at this point that this morning's gospel lesson really hits home. Jesus calls himself the gate or entrance for the sheep, the Good Shepherd (John 10:7, 9, 11; cf. 1 Peter 2:25; Psalms 23:1). He is the man who wants to lead you and me — to point us to the abundant life (John 10:10b). Jesus, the Good Shepherd, is putting his claim on you and me to be his sheep.

Of course, like you, I have heard the story of Jesus claiming to be the Good Shepherd hundreds of times in my life. However, I must confess that I never really heard it, never truly understood it, until I came to recognize that, "Hey, if Jesus is the Good Shepherd, I must be one of his sheep." Once I came to this realization, I began to realize that we, his followers, really are a lot like the sheep that Jesus was talking about. Think about his point! Do you remember what Jesus said about the matter?

First, recall, Jesus said that he was the only one whom the sheep would follow, because we sheep know his voice (John 10:3-5). Sometimes I wonder, however, whether this was not wishful thinking on Jesus' part. I call it wishful thinking, because those of you with roots on the farm know that sheep are not those warm, cuddly little animals that city people (like me) think they are. No, sheep are stubborn and willful. Martin Luther, one time when he was doing a sermon on the topic of the Good Shepherd, said that sheep "are most foolish and stupid animals."[3]

This was Jesus' point when he said that the sheep would not follow anyone else whom they did not know or trust (John 10:6). No, if a stranger comes, sheep will not follow that person; they will flee. You might say that they will "do their own thing." Sheep are pretty foolish, stubborn, selfish and willful creatures.

What do you folks think? I do not know about you folks, but I can see a little of myself in the sheep and their behavior. Really, do you not see a little of all of us in the way that those sheep act? I can see the similarities in the way that this community and American society in general often makes its decisions. Even we in this church often operate with the same decision-making criteria. We do things the way that we like it — the way it has always been done, or the new way, the business-like way, or whatever keeps people happy. Yes, those are the real criteria for our decision making. It is like how Peter put it in our second lesson. We have all been "straying like sheep (1 Peter 2:25)."

Doing it the way that we like it, just like sheep. We really are a lot like sheep. We have that stubborn, selfish streak in us. But are we living as Jesus' sheep? Are you letting him be your Good Shepherd? Is he guiding you, pointing you, giving you direction?

Friends, the story of the Good Shepherd is both making an invitation and stating some facts. People, it is saying, you really are sheep. You are stubborn, like sheep. You want what you like — even when what you like is not very good for you.

Is it not the truth? When you turn loose a herd of sheep, let them run wherever they desire, they are liable to run off a cliff — get themselves in all kinds of trouble. It is sort of like what can happen to us when we are making our decisions only on the basis of what we want to do. Some American social analysts have suggested that this is precisely the dynamic in American society today and helps explain some of the current malfunctionings of our system.[4]

People, like any herd of sheep, we need a shepherd — somebody to point us in the right directions, somebody to help us with our decisions. We already have somebody like that. But are we letting him guide us? Jesus Christ is applying for the job. In fact, on account of our baptisms, he already owns us! He can direct us to the good life, to life, to life abundant, to happiness (John 10:10b). Have we been listening?

We need to listen. We need to listen carefully to our Lord's Word, because, recall, sheep get scared of a stranger's voice. They will not pay any attention to the stranger's voice; they just do their own thing. Perhaps this has been one of your problems in this parish, and with mainline American Christianity in general. Jesus' voice, his words, his story, are not familiar enough to us! We only hear them Sunday mornings. We have not been asking enough what it is that Jesus and God want us to do.

It is true, is it not? In all of our parish meetings and activities, do we spend sufficient time and attention on asking what it is that Jesus and God want? Have we really let him be our Shepherd? No, too often here, as in virtually every congregation, Jesus' voice has been an unfamiliar one (for both the lay people and their pastor). We have been too inclined to do what we thought best, what we liked.

An active congregation like this one is wonderful. The involvement of such a large segment of our congregation in our decision-making can be a blessing. But it is only a blessing if we accept the invitation of the Good Shepherd, if we really let him lead, if we really rely on him in our decisions, if we are always asking what it is that God wants now.

Perhaps it is time in our parish council meetings, committee meetings, women's group and youth meetings, that we forgot about what we want — put aside a bit the questions of how we have always done it, what is good business, and the like. Perhaps it is time to put aside those concerns and, when there is a decision to be made, instead to ask what it is that God wants us to do. Perhaps we can find some directions concerning how we spend the church's money, how it gets raised, and the like, even in the Bible (of all places)! Perhaps we can find some answers or guidance to these particular questions by learning more about the teachings of the Christian faith.

In a way, I am putting in a call for a self-conscious commitment to improving our biblical literacy. However, I am also inviting us to consider a new attitude in our life together. (In part this attitude is a reflection of the new life given us in this Easter season by the resurrection.) In all our decisions in this community, from now on let us first ask the question of what Jesus wants, not what we want. In all our gatherings, perhaps it is time that we truly started letting Jesus be our Good Shepherd!

I am not just talking about the decisions that we make together as a community of Christ. I am also thinking about what goes on out there from Monday to Saturday in your life. Oh, not that the next time you have a big business deal coming up, or a hard day with the repairman and the kids, or a big test in school, all you need to do is to get a Bible out and start reading. No, that is not my proposal. It is not that simple. But in these situations it is perhaps time to ask Jesus to lead you. And as soon as you do that, as soon as you start asking what course of action might best please God, then forget yourself. Forget yourself, and let Jesus lead the way.

It is not a bad way to proceed; what do you think? The next time that you have a decision to make, maybe you ought to stop, just stop for a second, and ask yourself what God wants — really let Jesus lead. The promise of today's gospel lesson is that, to the degree that you let Jesus lead, life will be good and sweet, a little happier (John 10:10b). We have already been given that abundant new life with Jesus' resurrection. It is ours when we embrace Jesus in faith (Romans 6:2; 1 Peter 1:3). Being led by him is simply a matter of using, of living the life we already have been given.

The next time that you have a decision to make, give it some thought. Think about it; give Jesus a chance to lead you. How does he want to lead you? If we asked Jesus that question, I believe he would answer in something like the words that

Martin Luther once put in his mouth (in another sermon about Jesus as the Good Shepherd): "Therefore [Jesus says], joyfully abide with me and let none other rule in your consciences. Listen only to me, who speak and by deeds prove this comforting word, that I will not drive, trouble or burden you like Moses and the others, but will most lovingly lead and guide, protect and help you."[5]

"I will not drive, trouble or burden you [Jesus said], but will most lovingly lead and guide, protect and help you." He lovingly guides us. Who would not want a shepherd like Jesus?

**Easter 5
John 14:1-14 (C)
John 14:1-12 (L, RC)**
Focus Your Faith

"There are so many religions in the world. Everybody believes in God his/her own way. Consequently, it can't matter what you believe. That wouldn't be fair if it did! No, it does not matter what you believe; it's if you believe that counts. As long as you believe in something. That is what counts!"

"Ah, the church; who needs it? All you get there is a lot of hassles: Money-talk, changes, all those aggravating things. Hey, I want some peace; that is what I need! Heck, who can get close to God in the middle of all that mess? I can find God a whole lot better out in the fields (or in the mountains/at the beach) on Sunday mornings. You look up there in the sky, see the rolling hills and all the trees (or the waves), the deer; yeah, it is great. Just so peaceful; you really know there is a God."

Do these two different reflections sound familiar? Have you ever felt like these two friends of ours? I know that I have. In fact, I wager that you have, too. Competent social analysts tell us that this kind of religious individualism has all sorts of adherents in contemporary American society at the close of the century! Almost everybody has at least some periods in their life when they think that they can find God best on their own (in nature, through interactions with other people, in the goodness of life, in your own heart.)

I do not know how it stands for certain with you, but this is an awfully familiar road to me. I can tell you that I went through a period in my life — in my later teens and early 20s — when I just figured that all the religions of the world were equal. As long as you believed in something, that is all that counts. I thought that I could find God on my own, and as for the church — who needs it?

Perhaps some of you have never felt quite as strongly as I did. Perhaps you never reached the point where you thought that Christianity was just another religion. Just the same, however, have you ever wondered whether the church is really worth all the effort? Have you ever wondered whether we really need the Bible? Have you ever felt that you could find God on your own?

Be honest, now: Recall, we know each other pretty well. Of course, there have been times when you felt like you could find God on your own — without Jesus, without the Bible, without the church. Of course you have experienced times when you felt like you could just as well pray to God on your own — find him in nature or somewhere else.

Yes, we have those feelings on our own sometimes. This morning's gospel lesson really has something to say about such feelings. You remember the situation. This week's gospel lesson is taken from Jesus' farewell discourse.

It was the night of the last supper, and Jesus' disciples knew that something was up; they knew that Jesus was going to be betrayed by someone (John 13:21) and that he had plans to leave them (John 13:33; 14:3). They may not yet have grasped that he was preparing to die, but they were anxious (John 13:22, 36; 14:1). They did not know what to think. How could God possibly take Jesus away from them? It did not make any sense. How could God, our Heavenly Father, allow this to happen? How could he seem so cruel?

Jesus, the ever-caring man that he is, tried to calm his friends' anxiety (John 14:1). Think of it. The man is anxious about his own death (John 13:21), and yet he comforts others. What a loving, caring God we have! How can you not love someone like that?

Jesus assumed that his disciples knew where he was going (into heaven to prepare for them and his other followers [John 14:2-4]). But Thomas, ever the disciple full of questions, spoke for all of his friends when he asked Jesus where he was going and the way to get there (John 14:5). Then Jesus answered them: "I am the way, and the truth, and the life; no one comes to the Father, but by me (John 14:6)."

The disciples never could get it straight. Jesus has laid out everything we need, and we still do not get things straight. "Lord, show us the Father, and we shall be satisfied (John 14:8)," Philip said. It is rather like the questions we ask: "We want to know what God is really like, Jesus. We want to know why there is so much suffering, why you have to die, why do we?" And Jesus looked at them sadly and said: "He who has seen me has seen the Father . . . (John 14:9)." "The words that I say to you I do not speak on my own authority; but the Father who dwells in me does his works. Believe me that I am in the Father and the Father in me (John 14:10-11)." And Jesus said, "He who has seen me has seen the Father . . . (John 14:9)."

My friends, right here we have perhaps the deepest insight of the Christian faith. If we want to know who God is, if we want to know what he is really like, we already have our answer. The only answer is "Jesus Christ." Jesus shows who God is. For Jesus is God.

This is the core Christian commitment: Jesus is God. Whatever he says, whatever he does, it is God doing it. What is God like? He is the kind of a God who loved you and me so much, loved us so much, that he died for us. What is God like? He must really love us, for Jesus certainly did. Whoever has seen Jesus hanging on the cross has seen the Father, knows that God is so full of love that he would even die for us. We need to look for Jesus, to the Bible, to find out who God really is.

I hope that you caught the thrust of these questions and answers, because, if you did, now you know why one religion is not like any other. No, it does matter what you believe. Some of the other religions of the world may believe in God, but, because they do not know Jesus, they really do not know who God is. They do not know his great love.

It is no accident, you know, that in all of the religions of the world that I have studied, none of them speaks of God or the ultimate with quite the same stress on his love that Christianity does. Other religions, then, do not know who God is or what life is all about. They are trying. But they really do not know God's love. No other religion in the world talks about God's love as much as Christianity does. It really matters what you believe; if you do not believe in Jesus, you do not truly know God.

Oh, but there are other consequences to this Christian centeredness on Jesus. If you only truly know who God is because of Jesus, then you cannot find God just anywhere (without Jesus). You need Jesus, the Bible and the church.

Do not get me wrong. I am not rejecting the idea that God is in nature or out in the woods on Sunday morning. He is there. It is just that if that is the only place that you look for him, you do not know God aright.

Of course, the woods are beautiful on a nice spring day; God really seems good and loving. Yet what about when a forest fire hits? If that were all you had to go on, would God seem quite as loving? No, not very loving at all. How loving does God seem in the aftermath of a destructive earthquake or, to the farmer, in the midst of a wrenching drought? If that were all you had to go on, would you think that God is very loving then? No, we really only know who God is, when we come to Jesus and find him in his church.

Do not get me wrong. I am not saying that you cannot find God merely by praying to him in solitude. The only problem is that sometimes it just does not seem that God answers our prayers. Sometimes we do not seem to get what we asked. If that were all you had to go on, if that were all we knew about God (just by praying to him), then sometimes he would not seem very loving. Yes, we really only truly know who God is when our prayer life has been strengthened by looking to Jesus and his church.

Do not get me wrong. I am not saying that you cannot find God in life itself. How often we feel that life is really sweet, really good, and that God must be there in the middle of it. But sometimes life is not so sweet.

How about you? How about you when you have been knocked down by life? If the only thing that you knew about God was how life treated you, if that were all, then God would not seem too good. It really matters what you believe, or should I say in whom you believe. It matters. It is not enough merely to say that you believe in God, because you might not really know who God is at all if you are not careful.

Think about it: Is this not precisely what the Christian faith is proclaiming? We do not call ourselves "Godians" — people who merely believe in God. We are not "Godians." No, we are called by another name. We have been called Christians — "Christ-ians." That is, the world proclaims that we are people who only know who God is, because of Christ (Acts 11:26). From Jesus, the Jesus whom we meet in the Bible and in the church, we have the only way that we can truly know who God is. On our own we cannot know who God is; we need Jesus to make God known.

Martin Luther, as usual, made the same point so well in one of his sermons on the very gospel text that we are considering. Here is what he said: "This is the knowledge in which St. John, an outstanding evangelist with regard to this theme, and St. Paul instruct more than the others do. They join and bind Christ and the Father so firmly together that we learn to think of God only as Christ. As soon as we hear the mention of God's name, or of his will, his works, his grace, or his displeasure, we must not judge these as the voice of our heart or man's wisdom discourse on them . . . but we must nestle and cuddle on the lap of Christ, like dear children on their mother's lap or in her arms, and close our eyes and ears to everything but him and his words."[2]

Just cuddle up on Christ's lap. Don't get Luther and me wrong at this point. We are not saying that you cannot find God in nature, or in your prayers, or in life. We are not making that claim. We are merely saying that if this is all the data that you have, you cannot quite be sure that there is a loving God. For there are things in life that do not seem so beautiful.

Jesus is rather like a pair of glasses, a pair of glasses that we need to wear. Without them, you do not quite see things correctly. Yet once you are wearing them, then you can truly see God in all the realms of life. Then you can really see him in all his love. However, if you do not wear them, if you do not put them on much, like people who think that they do not need Jesus or his church, but can find God somewhere else, then you are not really wearing your glasses. In that case, you are not really seeing God; you don't really know him.

If you just look at nature or the way life is going, you cannot be quite sure. There are just too many "maybes." That is why we need Jesus and his church to make us sure that God loves us. Right here, my friends, in our worship, in the proclaimed word, in the bread, wine, and water of the sacraments, you meet a God who loves you so much that he died for you. That is the way God really is: Jesus shows us. Go and cuddle up on his lap, and close your eyes and ears to everything else. We have a God who is so loving that you can cuddle up to him, so loving that he died for you. With Jesus for your glasses, showing you the way, you cannot miss that loving God! Along with the psalmist, that kind of love makes you want to praise the Lord, sing a new song (Psalm 33:2-3), for "the earth is full" of his steadfast love (Psalms 33:5).

**Easter 6
John 14:15-21**

Good Works Will Not Save You!

Jesus was still in the middle of his farewell discourse to his disciples. He was trying to comfort the despair that they were feeling when they had first heard the news (during the last supper) that Jesus would be leaving them (John 13:21, 33; 14:1). He had comforted them with the good news that he was on the way to God the Father, that in associating with Jesus, the disciples had been in fellowship with the Father (John 14:6-11). Whoever believed in him, Jesus said, would be able to do the works that he had done, even greater works (John 14:12). In fact, he added, "if you ask anything in my name, I will do it (John 14:13)."

After these words of comfort, Jesus uttered some words that seem a lot less comforting to me. First, he said: "If you love me you will keep my commandments (John 14:15)." Then, after offering some comforting words about the Holy Spirit whom he would send in his place so that the disciples would not be desolate in his absence (John 14:16-20), Jesus offered another most troubling reflection: "He who has my commandments and keeps them [Jesus said], he it is who loves me; and he who loves me will be loved by my Father, and I will love him . . . (John 14:21)."

Whoever keeps my commandments loves me [Jesus], and such a person will be loved by the Father. Is Jesus suggesting here that God only loves us if we keep his commandments? If so, we are all in a lot of trouble. No one in this building (at least not the guy in the pulpit) is measuring up on that score. The Bible itself teaches us that "All have sinned and fall short of the glory of God," Paul says (Romans 3:23). None of us seems to keep the commandments sufficiently to earn God's love. Consequently, what can Jesus mean? It is as if his resurrection on Easter had not changed a thing. We seem still to be obligated to fulfill God's law, and we are powerless to do what the law of God commands.

Thank God, though, that things have changed because of Easter. Jesus talks about the gift of the Holy Spirit that he is giving his followers (John 14:16-18). But what good will that do us? How has the gift of the Holy Spirit made us different from the old selfish sinners we have always been? Besides, where is the Holy Spirit? We have no extraordinary manifestations of the Spirit, no miracles happening, in this church. What are we to make of Jesus' words?

No doubt about it, between references to the Holy Spirit and to keeping the commandments, we have a difficult text on our hands. Yet Jesus also points us to some fruitful insights about these matters, to a helpful image for understanding our daily Monday through Saturday walk of faith. First he says that, though the world cannot see nor understand the Holy Spirit, nevertheless, the spirit will be in us (John 14:17). Next Jesus proceeds to comfort the disciples and us with these words: "I will not leave you desolate [he says]; I will come to you. Yet a little while, and the world will see me no more, but you will see me; because I live, you will know that I am in my Father, and you in me, and I in you (John 14:18-20)."

"You are in me," he says, "and I am in you." Just as Jesus is in the Father, so the believer and Jesus have a similar intimate relationship. You and Jesus have that kind of relationship going. You might say that you are living together.

Living together. The image connotes intimacy. The sort of intimacy and sharing of body and soul which happens between human beings committed to each other (an intimacy finding its highest human expression in marriage).

Think with me about the most intimate relationship you have had with another human being — with a spouse, with a parent, with a teacher, with a dear friend (to whom you are not related). What is it like for you to share in that relationship? It is beautiful, is it not? You have shared so deeply in the life of the person you love, he or she shares so fully in your life, that it is almost impossible to think of yourself without that partner. You understand the experience to which I refer at this point, do you not?

I think of how it is with Betsey and me. When the family is engaged in some new activity or way of doing business, sometimes you forget whose idea it was originally. In my own work, I come up with a new insight or write it down. But was the idea really originally mine? Of course it is my idea; I just thought it. But was the idea not first something I received from the latest book I read and loved? Was it not first inspired by one of my teachers? Or did it emerge from a conversation with Betsey? Did she first suggest it? I am not certain. Her idea — my idea; my teacher's thought or mine? That is the sort of intimacy and sharing that emerges in a close relationship. Of course, with spouses, it is especially intense. Probably that is because they are together so much. It happens from living together (sometimes being in one another).

Jesus says that he has that kind of relationship with the Father. They live together! But miracle of miracles, he has that sort of relationship with you and me. You and he, he and I, live together, sharing the kind of intimacies (even deeper) that you and your spouse (or you and your closest friend) share. Everything you and Christ have is common property — the good, as well as the evil.[1] (No pre-nuptual agreement here.) Christ takes our sin. In return, we receive all that he has — his righteousness and his love. The founder of the Reformed/Presbyterian churches, John Calvin, said it so well in his most important book. Here is what he said; referring to our growth into one body with Christ, he writes: "As a consequence [of our growth into one body with Christ], we may dare assure ourselves that eternal life, of which he [Christ] is the heir, is ours . . . This is the wonderful exchange which out of his [Christ's] measureless benevolence, he has made with us; that, becoming Son of man with us, he has made us sons of God with him . . . that, accepting our weakness he has strengthened us by his power; that, receiving our poverty unto himself; he transferred his wealth to us; that, taking the weight of our iniquity upon himself (which oppressed us), he has clothed us with his righteousness."[2]

Everything that Christ has is yours and mine. The works that he has done, you can do (John 14:12). It comes with living together.

In today's lesson, Jesus says that the faithful also will receive the Holy Spirit along with Christ (John 14:16-17). Later in his farewell discourse, he refers to the Holy Spirit again and says that the Spirit will "bring [Christ] to . . . remembrance (John 14:26)." The work of the Holy Spirit is related to uniting the faithful with Christ. The Spirit works in making you and Christ live together.

For me, this way of understanding the work of the Holy Spirit makes the Holy Spirit a lot less threatening and a lot less difficult to understand (and find). The Holy Spirit and his work are not limited to extraordinary manifestations (natural miracles). The Holy Spirit brings Christ to live in you and me (John 14:16-17).

The work of the Holy Spirit makes even more sense when you think about the relationship that you have with Jesus in terms of a relationship of two people in love who live together. Think about that with me. There is something mysterious, almost miraculous about the love-relationships in which you share with the person or people closest to you. The bonding that brings lives together is not natural; it is extraordinary.

I am not so great that I deserve having someone's life tied up in mine forever. Of myself I do not have the capacity and loyalty to stick with someone else for better or for worse forever. Yet it happens! Bonding and sharing between two people happens. The love that emerges in these kinds of relationships is truly miraculous.

All the more miraculous it is that you and I now have that kind of relationship with Jesus. We are living together with him. It is truly miraculous! The miracle is the work of the Holy Spirit.

You wonder where the Holy Spirit is? You wonder why the Spirit does not seem to be among us working his miracles? The Holy Spirit is among us, working miracles, whenever we believe in Jesus and (miracle of miracles) whenever he makes his home with us. Martin Luther said it so profoundly in a sermon he once gave on our gospel text for today. He puts these words in Jesus' mouth: "You should not be guided by such feelings or believe your own thoughts [Luther had Jesus say]; you should believe my Word. For I will ask the Father, and as a result of my plea he will surely give you the Holy Spirit to comfort you. Then you can rest assured that I love you, that the Father loves you, and that the Holy Spirit, who is sent to you, loves you.

"Your heart will counter: 'You have not been living right; you are full of sin.' Unfortunately, this is all too true . . . [But] my Lord Christ . . . tells me that the Father is not angry with me but will give me the Comforter, who will come to me in answer to his prayer. They concur in this, that they do not want me to be frightened and sad, much less rejected and condemned, but comforted and happy . . .

"It is correct to teach that the Holy Spirit is called the Comforter . . ."[3]

The Holy Spirit is certainly a miracle worker. As the Holy Spirit, God gives us comfort in the midst of our despair and anguish about the ups and downs of life — about the times when Jesus and God seem to be absent. He brings us Christ who, with the Father, has become your daily guest, a true member of your household![4] For Christ is living with you.

Whenever you experience Christ's presence in your life, whenever you catch yourself doing good because it is somehow the result of Jesus' good influence rubbing off on you, that is the work of the Holy Spirit. Any time we believe and do good, the Holy Spirit is present. It is a miracle!

There is no need for us to wonder about the Holy Spirit and where he is in our lives. The Spirit is very much alive in our church and in your life. His miraculous work is happening whenever God's work is being done through us. Every good we do, all our faith, is the Spirit's work.

Although we have dealt with the problem of where the Holy Spirit is, we still have that other big problem in our text to face. We still have to straighten out what Jesus could have meant when he seemed to say that whoever keeps the commandments loves Christ and so will be loved by the Father and the Son (John 14:21). Is God's love for us contingent on our doing good works?

That is not Jesus' point at all. Such good works are merely a natural consequence of living with Jesus. Good works come naturally when you live with someone you love.

Think once again of those with whom you live and/or love. It is not hard to be nice to them, is it?

It is not that the loving actions I show to Betsey are the result of my good heart and unselfishness. It is more like I am captive of her good qualities and her love. They rub off on me. That is the way it is for us Christians in our life together with Jesus. His goodness and his love for us rubs off on us, and we do good works.

Suppose it never happened? Suppose I did not ever show good deeds of love to Betsey? Would it not seem like I did not love her? The loving deeds you do naturally for the one you live with and love show your love for your lover. Yes, if we love Jesus, we will spontaneously keep his commandments (John 14:15).

Love is a blessed (not vicious) circle. Just as Betsey finds me a bit more lovable when I show her my love, by my deeds, so God loves us when we show him our love (John 14:21).

Yet just as it is not the loving deeds you do for your mate that makes her (or him) love you originally (because the loving deeds I do for Betsey are a response to her love), so God loves us first. That is the cause of the good works that we do. Before good works can be done, Jesus and the Father first come and live with us!

As usual, Martin Luther said it so well: "But, as Christ said earlier, it all depends on whether you feel and find that you love this man [Jesus]. For if you truly believe this, then love will be there, and your heart will be moved to say: 'Christ, my dear Lord, has done so much for me. He has reconciled the Father to me and shed his blood for me. He has fought and defeated my death and given me all his possessions. Should I not requite this love? Should I not thank, praise, honor and serve him with my life and my goods? If not, I should be ashamed that I am a human being.'

"Therefore Christ declares: 'Sincere love for me is part of a true Christian.' "[5]

When you believe in Christ, when you live with him, love and good works just naturally flow. They come from living together with Christ; his good influence just rubs off on us.

Of course, the good works will not save you. They do not merit God's love or win you "brownie points" with him. The good works stem first from God's love. They result from the fact that in his resurrection we have been given a new life. The Spirit and Christ live in us (John 14:17, 20). Good works come naturally with live-in partners like that.

When you love someone and live with them, works of love just come naturally. Jesus is living with you. His good influence is rubbing off on you. Good works and a new life are coming! They just come naturally when you live with Jesus. And he certainly is living with all of us.

Easter 7
John 17:1-11

The Majesty Of God's Love

Jesus was drawing near to the end of his farewell discourse to his disciples, a sermon he gave to them (according to John) on the evening of the last supper. In our gospel lesson for today, Jesus broke into a prayer to the Father. It is a famous prayer called the high priestly prayer. There are many spiritual riches to mine in this prayer and our text. For our purposes today on this last Sunday of Easter, the Sunday after the festival of Jesus' ascension into heaven with the church's celebration of the Trinity not far off, the last sentence of our lesson for today is especially crucial to us.

Jesus had been talking to his disciples about life after he left them (John 14:2-3, 18). By the time he got to the prayer in our lesson for today, he was addressing the theme of his glorification (John 17:1). Of course, Jesus' glorification happened both at the resurrection and again in the ascension. Consequently the prayer speaks to our situation on this Sunday of the Easter season, the Sunday after the ascension. Here is what Jesus prayed: "Holy Father [he prayed], keep them [my followers] in thy name, which thou hast given me, that they may be one, even as we are one (John 17:11b)."

Make my followers one, as we are one. A whole cluster of themes jump out at us. Jesus wants his followers to be one, like he and the Father are one.

This notion of the Father and Son being one, especially at this time in the church year when we celebrate the ascension, is bound to lead us to consider God in all his glory and majesty (the Triune God). Not just the Father and the Son, but along with the Holy Spirit, the three make one. How can these three make one? Jesus says it is in the same way that all of us believers are one. How can that be the case?

Making one out of three, explaining the Trinity, has always been a real challenge to the church. We have not usually done a very good job. And we have not been very successful in making the Trinity a crucial aspect in the everyday life of the faithful. Seriously folks, if the Trinity doctrine were discarded next week by an ecumenical council (kind of like the council that drew up the Nicene Creed), would your faith really be affected? Would it make that much of a difference to you in your daily Monday through Saturday life?

I think that we all know the answer. And it is a tragedy, a judgment on the church, that we have not learned the lesson that the Trinity and Jesus' high priestly prayer teach. They teach us an important lesson about the majesty of God's love.

The majesty of God's love. For me the love of God and its relationship to the Trinity has been best explained by an African theologian of the earliest centuries, a man named Augustine. Augustine took very seriously the idea that our God is a God who wants his people to love in a special way. What is that special way? The Bible teaches it. In marriage, it claims, God wants love to make one out of two (two become one) (Ephesians 5:31; Genesis 2:24). He wants love to make many become one. (Human love at its best works that way. In any family unit to which you have belonged, the love you have for the other members of that family made you all one with them — one family.)

Of course we love that way because God is love. God's love is the perfect love. In him, the many (the three) become one. Here is how Augustine explained it.[1]

We begin with the Father. The Father is eternal, with a burning desire to love. The Father cannot help himself. He is so full of love. Yet in eternity, what does he have to love? Consequently, God posited himself again as an other, as an object of his love. He posited himself again as the Son. Therefore, in eternity, forever and ever, God the Father has had someone to love. He had the Son.

For Jesus' high priestly prayer (today's gospel lesson) we are reminded that everything that the Son has is from the Father (John 17:7). Likewise, all that the Son has he gives back to the Father (John 17:10). The Father is love, overwhelming love. All that he has, the Son has. Consequently, the Son is likewise love — majestic, overwhelming love. He loves the Father back.

In eternity, forever and ever, Father and Son have loved each other. They could not stop themselves. Long before creation, long before they had something else to love, the Father and the Son were consumed by a burning desire to love something. Thus, they needed each other to love. In eternity, the Father loved the Son, and their love was mutual.

Do we have here two gods — God the Father and God the Son? It is at this point that Augustine introduced the role of the Holy Spirit. The Holy Spirit, who, according to the Nicene Creed, "proceeds from the Father and the Son." According to Augustine, the Holy Spirit is the love that binds them together. Augustine's words in describing this phenomenon are beautiful. Here is what he wrote: "Therefore the Holy Spirit, whatever it is, is something common both to Father and Son. But that communion itself is consubstantial and coeternal; and it may fitly be called friendship, let it be so called; but it is aptly called love. And this is also a substance, and 'God is love . . .' "[2]

The Holy Spirit is the love that binds Father and Son together as One. The Father loves the Son and the Spirit is the love that makes them One. That is the Trinity.

Even, and especially, in himself, God's love makes one out of many. In his high priestly prayer, Jesus prays that his followers like us would be one, even as God himself is One (John 17:11b). Yet, how can that be? Is not Jesus being a bit unrealistic? He could not intend that all of us lose our individual separateness, become one in the sense that Father, Son and Spirit are One, could he?

Of course, none of us can love like God. Only his love is perfect. Only his love can literally make one out of many.

In a good marriage, two become one to a great extent. It is not that the marriage dissolves the separateness of the partners. But they truly do become one in the sense that the marriage becomes more important than the partners as individuals. That is the kind of relationship which Jesus prays that his followers might have with each other. It just comes naturally when you worship a triune God.

At this point, the importance of the Trinity for our daily life here at church and in the world becomes evident. In the Trinity we live with a God who is so full of love that his love makes one out of many. Of course, such love is contagious. As Christians we may catch some of it and likewise be driven to love the many into one — to relate to all of the followers of Christ as if we were one.

You hear a lot about ecumenism and Christian unity from time to time. This drive towards becoming truly one church is rooted right here in the scripture, specifically as a consequence of the Trinity. The next time that you do not feel excited about ecumenical efforts, the next time that you are critical of efforts to unify the churches, give some thought to the Trinity and see if you do not conclude that our triune God wants his people to be one. Not that he might want one united union church. God's oneness does not abolish the distinctions between Father, Son and Holy Spirit. Perhaps God is calling for a unity of Christians like his own internal unity. Perhaps he wants us to maintain our separate (denominational) identities in a united church (just as the distinct identities of his three persons are maintained in the unity of the Trinity).[3] In any case, the nature of God as three in one demands that we, his people, be one.

Faith in a triune God entails that there is no such thing as an individualistic Christian faith, one unconcerned about relationships in society or relationships among Christians. One well-known conservative Evangelical theologian put it this way: "Trinitarian religion involves all man's relations to God and to society; the social relationships within the Trinity call out against any antisocial interpretation of personal religion."[4]

A triune God who is always yearning to bring the many into one wants his people to be that way, too. He wants people who are yearning to help make all human beings one people (John 17:18-21). Don't you yearn for it, too? Believing in the Trinity has all sorts of practical implications about the way you live your life. How dare we say we believe in a God whose love is so great that it makes one out of many, if we also do not, year after year, live as though we and all people were one? It is a little wonder that Jesus prayed that his people might be one.

What did he mean by praying for our oneness? I have found a helpful image in one of the sermons of Martin Luther. In an Easter sermon that he gave in 1538, Luther claimed that all Christians are formed in a common brotherhood insofar as they share a common inheritance.[5] We share a common inheritance (namely, salvation and eternal life — the majestic love of the triune God).

A common inheritance. The image makes me think of a family. Think of your own family. You and all the members of your family share a common inheritance — common family ties, common genes, common stories, perhaps even common values and material possessions. My children, Elizabeth, Peter and Pat, seem to be three very different characters. Elizabeth will always be the boys' sister, no matter what happens. All three have been cursed with a common gene pool. They will have common stories about childhood that they can swap with each other for the rest of their lives (even if they went their separate ways). These children, their parents, and their three living grandparents, are one.

It is in this sense that Jesus prayed that all his people, including you and me, would be one. He wants us to revel in the common inheritance that we share — our common creaturehood and the majestic love that God has for us. That love, in particular, is the common inheritance that binds us together — makes us one family.

Indeed, we have a God who is literally full of love. It is a love so majestic that it made him discontent to be alone. Consequently God posited himself again as Son, and his love was so dynamic that it made God One again.

Such love is not content. It created us. It died for us (to redeem us from sin and evil). It is making us new — making us one. A love that will not quit until it makes us one family.

What a rich common inheritance you and I, all Christians and all creatures, share. We share in the love of the triune God — a love that makes one out of many. This love is what Easter and the new life given in the resurrection is all about. This love is what the ascension of Jesus into heaven is all about, too. For though Jesus has gone to be with the Father in glory, through the Holy Spirit his love is present among us. By making us one, he is giving us over to the Father, to God in all his majesty. Be awake to your (new) inheritance, people. The triune God has a love so majestic that he cannot fail to make us one. That love has been made manifest. Let us go now and live that way — as a people whom God has made into one family!

Ascension Day/Ascension Sunday (C, L)
Luke 24:46-53 (C)
Luke 24:44-53 (L)

What Makes Those Disciples So Darn Happy?

"I tell you, those disciples had it made! I sure wish that I had been alive in those days. They had it easy. It could not have been very hard for them to believe in Jesus and in God. They had it made! They had Jesus with them all of the time. It is harder for us, because we do not have Jesus; he is with the Father. Consequently, we have to believe in him; faith is all we've got. But the disciples had him present with them. What a gyp! It really is difficult being a Christian when all you have going for you is faith. If only we had known Jesus like those disciples did. Yes, then believing in him would not be so difficult!"

Have you ever felt this way? I know that I have. Because I have felt these feelings, the big church festival which we celebrate today (the ascension of Jesus into heaven) was never much of a celebration for me. In fact, it was a real "downer." The ascension, bah, who needs it?

Who needs it? If Jesus had not ascended into heaven, we would still have him among us. That would be great! What is so "hot" about the ascension? It seems like we ought to be sad about it, because we lost Jesus on that day. He is not with us anymore.

Have you ever felt that way? Probably you have. If you have, then the ascension is no big deal to you. It is nothing to get very excited about. However, people, let me tell you. We really have been missing out. The ascension really is a great thing for us Christians. Today is a great day, people. Get happy, for Jesus has gone home to be with his Father. What a great day!

Do not misunderstand me; I am not trying to get rid of Jesus. No, not at all. It is just that today is a great day, because the ascension is a day of victory for our God. Jesus has conquered everything — sin, death, evil, everything. Now he has gone home to be with God. He has put on the glory that belongs to him. This is a great day of victory, a real homecoming for Jesus. And since Jesus is our friend, somebody we love, it is only natural that we should share the joy that the disciples felt when he left them (Luke 24:52); we ought to be joyful with them — happy for our friend.

However, people, there is something else for us to rejoice about today. The ascension is not just a wonderful day for Jesus and God; something great happens to us today as well. There is something that is great in it for us. To be sure, today is Jesus' great day of victory; today he truly puts on the glory that belongs to him; he goes to be with the Father. Yet today is also our day of victory as well!

Let me explain: When Jesus, the Son of God, ascended into heaven, he was not exactly the same as when he left. Of course, he was basically the same, but just a little bit different. He left as the eternal Son of God to become a man on earth. He came back as the eternal Son of God, but he also came back to the Father as the man Jesus.

Think about this point for a moment, folks; think about it with me. When Jesus returned to heaven, as he ascended, he did not throw his body back on the earth. Of course, it was as the Son of God that he returned to the Father, but as the Son of God who is also the man Jesus.

Jesus, the Son of God, returned home to the Father to be with the Father forever and ever. Never more to be separated, for they are one. Think about it: the man, the human being named Jesus, has returned to the Father forever and ever, never more to part.

This entails that part of God's very nature, part of the way that he is henceforth, is that one cannot escape us human beings. From now on, he and Jesus are one; God is one with a man, the man Jesus. The man Jesus, a man in many ways like you and me, is so wrapped up in God that together they are one. This is what the doctrine of the Trinity is really proclaiming. Henceforth, because Jesus and the Father are one, there is a little bit of you and me (thanks to Jesus), a little human streak, in God. There is no way that God can reject it; it is part of who he is. From now on, God can never really be God unless he is all wrapped up in a human being, because, after all, they are one. No, God really cannot be himself unless he is all wrapped up in people.

This is why the ascension is such a great thing for you and me. You see, we have been promised that whatever happened to this man Jesus, will happen to us if we believe it (John 14:12). This is what our baptism is all about; in our baptisms we all became one with Jesus. As he rose from the dead on Easter, so someday we shall rise from the dead (Romans 6:3-6). This also implies that just as Jesus and the Father are one, so because we are one with Jesus, we, too, are one with the Father (1 John 4:15). God cannot get rid of us!

One could almost say that, since he has that human streak in him because of Jesus, there is something about God's personality that he cannot be himself unless he is all wrapped up in the lives of human beings. He is one with Jesus, and since in baptism we are one with Jesus, so God is stuck with us. Because he has that little streak of Jesus' human nature in him, God has just got to be with us people — with you and me. He has to immerse himself in our lives, or he just is not being himself.

He is immersed in our lives, you know. He is with us right here and now. That is what the Holy Spirit, whom Jesus promised to his disciples before ascending to heaven (Luke

24:49), is all about. God is the Holy Spirit among us, because he just cannot keep his "nose" out of our lives.

People, I do not know about you, but once I think about the ascension in that manner, there is no way that I would ever be sorry that Jesus ascended to heaven. I am glad he did. In fact, if Jesus were physically standing here right in front of me, I would ask him to get going — to get back to the Father. Why? Because by being with the Father, by being one with the Father, it is almost like Jesus' human nature acts like a constant reminder to God that he is stuck with us. He cannot really be himself without us. You see, however, none of this would have happened if Jesus had just remained right here on earth.

"Oh," but you say, "it would be so nice to have Jesus here now with us; it would make it easier to believe. The disciples had it easy; they had him among them." Well, people, let me tell you; we have Jesus among us right here — plain as day.

If Jesus had not ascended into heaven, God would not be with us in all of the good things of life that we experience. At least we could not be certain that he is with us in those events. There would always be that doubt that maybe they were all accidents, not a consequence of God's actions. Perhaps we might be led to conclude that it is only an accident that Betsey and the rest of my family love me (or that the loves in which you are engaged are merely accidents). Yet that is not the case. God has his hand in all of these events; indeed Jesus (through the Holy Spirit) is in the middle of that love and of all the good things in our lives.

Open your eyes, my friends! God is among us; he has willed not to be fully himself any longer without us. It sure is great that Jesus has ascended. Now he is free (through the Spirit) to be ever among us in a way that he could not have done as effectively had he remained on earth in visible bodily form! It sure is great that he ascended, so that he could always be with us after all.

Ascension Day / Ascension Sunday (RC)
Matthew 28:16-20 (RC)
The Majesty Of God's Love

Today we celebrate Jesus' ascension into heaven. Our gospel lesson from Matthew does not directly speak of our Lord's ascension, but it does provide some clues regarding its significance. It has to do with Jesus' great commission ("to make disciples of all nations [Matthew 28:19])" and its relationship to the Trinity. Somehow Jesus' ascension represents an internal divine commitment by God that he will not quit until everyone is wrapped up in his love.

Here is the story. According to Matthew's version, on that first Easter the angel instructed the women at the empty tomb to tell the disciples of Jesus that they should go to Galilee to meet the Risen Lord there (Matthew 28:7). Jesus repeated the request when he appeared to the women later that morning (Matthew 29:8-10). Of course, the region of Galilee included the town of Nazareth. (Capernaum was also located in the region.) Thus it was Jesus' home area, and many of his disciples had their roots in that region. Consequently, it was quite natural that Jesus would arrange to be reunited with his disciples on their home turf.

Obediently, though apparently with some skepticism about reports concerning Jesus' resurrection, the disciples immediately left Jerusalem after learning of the angel's directive and headed for Galilee (Matthew 28:16-17). And then in our lesson, Jesus appeared to them on a mountain in Galilee (Matthew 28:16-17). There is some debate among scholars concerning where Jesus came from in this appearance. Was it merely another of his resurrection appearances here on earth? Or had he been associating with the heavenly presence of the Father before the appearance?[1]

The report that when the disciples saw Jesus, they worshiped him (Matthew 28:17) suggests that somehow the glory of God was emanating from him. The disciples had not previously worshiped him, and in none of the other resurrection appearances in any of the gospels is the Risen Christ worshiped. Yet in this account he is worshiped. Does this not connote that Jesus' glorified, divine nature was shining through his earthly body? The disciples were perhaps getting a glimpse of Jesus' heavenly presence (sort of like they had at the transfiguration [Matthew 17:1ff; Mark 9:2ff; Luke 9:28ff].) Some have even speculated that the Galilean mountain on which Jesus appeared to his disciples in our story (Matthew 28:16) is exactly the same mountain on which he was transfigured (Matthew 17:1, et al.). This would support the idea that we should understand today's gospel story, like we do the transfiguration, as a revelation of Jesus' heavenly glory.[2] In a way, then, this resurrection appearance points us to the theme of the day — to the ascension; to the way Jesus is continuing to relate to us as he sits in his heavenly glory after the ascension.

There are more clues in Matthew's gospel that today's gospel lesson is properly read in relation to Jesus' ascension. It is, after all, the very end of the gospel. No further events in Jesus' earthly life are recorded by Matthew. Can we not, then, rightly assume that he was soon to ascend? After all, he promises to be evermore with the disciples (Matthew 28:20). Yet we know that this was not the case with regard to Jesus' bodily presence with the disciples. (Think of his bodily absence in Acts.) Consequently, unless Jesus was lying, his promise to be with the disciples (Matthew 28:20) must refer to the sense in which he would be present with them spiritually after his ascension.

Jesus is reported to have said some other things to suggest that he should be understood in this story in light of his ascension into heaven. After all, he spoke to the disciples in a way as if he were saying good-bye to them — giving them directives concerning their future mission (Matthew 28:19-20). In addition, he also seemed to refer to the heavenly glory and majesty that he shares with the Father, as he referred to the Trinity (to baptism in the name of the Father, Son and Holy Spirit) (Matthew 28:19). Yes, there are all sorts of indications that we should understand today's gospel lesson in light of how we are to live now that Jesus has ascended.

The punchline to it all comes at the end of Jesus' remarks to his followers. To them he said: "Go therefore and make disciples of all nations, baptizing them in the name of the Father and of the Son and of the Holy Spirit, teaching them to observe all that I have commanded you; and lo, I am with you always, to the close of the age (Matthew 28:19-20)."

Jesus commissions the disciples and us to baptize. He invokes the Trinity. Then he proceeds to assure us that he will not be totally absent from us. Jesus' ascension brings us to the threshold of some of the deepest mysteries of our faith.

The ascension. What do you make of it? To be sure, it explains why Jesus is no longer bodily present with us (except in the sacraments). But why is it a festival? What is there to celebrate? It would be a whole lot nicer for us if Jesus were still around in the body, a whole lot easier to believe in him, right?

We have something to celebrate about in Jesus' ascension. His glorification in heaven is our assurance that nothing can ultimately harm us. He has all authority on heaven and earth (Matthew 28:18). One of the 16th century Protestant reformers expressed the Catholic faith very well at this point. Here is what he said: "For while my enemies stand before my very door and plan to slay me, my faith reasons thus: Christ is ascended into heaven and became Lord over all creatures, hence my enemies, too, must be subject to him and thus it is not in their power to do me harm."[3]

With Jesus in heaven, a sure sign that he is Lord of all, those of us who are in him can be assured that nothing ultimately can harm us. Are you in the midst of temptation? Do you fear what comes next? Christ is Lord over all suffering, temptation and evil. Have confidence that, because you are in him, and under the care of his lordship, none of these ultimately can harm you. The ascension of Jesus, then, is the assurance that Jesus is caring for us when we are down. Hang on to it the next time that you are suffering; the ascension really is something to celebrate.

Oh, but the ascension is more. It points us to the majesty of the Trinity and serves as a seal to the fact that God in his triune majesty has a human side. What an assuring, comforting word. It explains even more fully the great commission that Jesus gave us to evangelize the world. The ascension unambiguously certifies that God has a human side and wants us dearly. Think about it with me.

Jesus' ascension into heaven seems to have been with a body (Acts 1:9). United in essence with the Father, he gives to the Father all that is his (including, presumably, the body). This entails that part of God's very being, part of the way that he is henceforth, is that he cannot escape us human beings. From now on, at least since the ascension, he and Jesus are one. The man Jesus, a man in many ways like you and me, is so wrapped up in God that together they form one.

Their union is even more perfect. The Holy Spirit, who according to Augustine, is the blessed love between Father and Son, makes them one.[4] The Father loves the Son and the Spirit makes them one. That is the Trinity doctrine in a nutshell. Insofar as the ascension of Jesus entails that this oneness includes a human component, God can not be God unless he is all wrapped up in the lives of human beings (for the Son with whom he is one is such a human).

Here we see what is really at stake for God in the great commission to make disciples of all nations (Matthew 28:19). Reunited with the man Jesus in his ascension, it is God's very nature to seek union with human beings. In the work of evangelism (in bringing others to faith in him), God is truly "doing his thing." He is becoming more of what he already is — a God who is all tied up in the fate of humanity.

Likewise, when we take up Jesus' great commission, when we do evangelism, we are merely doing our own thing. The fact that baptism is in the name of the Trinity reminds us of that (Matthew 28:19). The ascension and baptism in the name of the Trinity can be wonderful supports to us in our evangelism efforts. Let me explain that point.

Evangelism. It is a word on every pair of American Christian lips these days. Everyone is speaking of church growth. Yes, we all talk about it, but it does not come easy in action. All of us, your priest included, know the difficulties and the awkwardness that come when you try to talk about the Catholic faith. The going gets even tougher when we try to excite faith in others or endeavor to encourage them to practice the faith. Evangelism is a real choice; it just seems so unnatural and imposing a task sometimes.

It is precisely at this point that the ascension and the invocation of the Trinity can be such supports to us in our evangelism efforts. We have a God for whom evangelism (gathering human beings together in faith) just comes naturally. It is part of who he is. But insofar as you and I have been baptized into Christ (baptized, as it were, into the Trinitarian relationships of the Son with the Father and the Spirit), we have received all that Christ and God has (Romans 6:3-6; John 14:12). Consequently, evangelism ought to come just as naturally to us as it does to Jesus and God. Insofar as we are wrapped up in Christ and he in the Trinity (John 14:20), God's concern about human beings and their spiritual relationship with him is our concern. Evangelism, you might say, is in our blood.

The real you and me (the one created in our baptisms, the new being that is ours in the Easter resurrection) shares that concern for the evangelism, for the spiritual well-being of our brothers and sisters. We will receive a "booster shot;" more of that attitude will be getting into our blood in just a few moments, as we receive Christ into our bodies through the eucharist. Just as the Father through his union with Christ is tied up with a concern for the spiritual welfare of humanity, so we, the faithful, insofar as we are united with Christ, share the Trinitarian concern to reach all with the gospel.

When you are being true to the kind of person God has made you (in Christ's resurrection and in your baptism), then evangelism is no odious task. You do it with enthusiasm. It just comes naturally.

This is why Jesus directs us to baptize in the name of the triune God (Matthew 28:19). The reference to the Trinity reminds us that our efforts to bring others to Christ just come naturally to those who believe in a triune God. By the same token, those who are baptized are taken into fellowship with a God and fellow-believers who are by nature evangelists.

Evangelism may seem like a strained awkward activity for us in many situations, something like a burden hung around our necks. Jesus' ascension, which places his humanity (and therefore our humanity) in union with the Trinity, is a reminder that we are so tied up with an evangelizing Lord that evangelism is just part of who we are. It is rather like having a dear friend or family member who loves a particular activity (let us say baseball). Taking such a loved one to a ball game is no demanding chore. It just comes naturally. It is the same for Christians in responding to the "evangelizing" triune God to whom we are linked.

Yes, evangelism has been put in your "spiritual blood" in virtue of your union with Christ through your faith and your baptism. It is no burdensome task when we are being true to the new life that Christ has given you. That awareness will help free you up when you are doing evangelism. It has freed me. It gives us confidence to do evangelism; it is a motivator. But there is one more freeing word that the ascension speaks concerning evangelism. That word is right here in our gospel text. Jesus says to the disciples and to us: ". . . lo I am with you always, to the close of the age (Matthew 28:20b)."

The Holy Spirit makes Christ present to us (John 14:16, 17; 1 John 4:13; Romans 8:9). We are not alone when we do evangelism. Jesus is manifest and doing it with us! Evangelism is surely no burden when we keep in mind that our Lord is doing it with us.

The ascension is a great festival. It makes evangelism a joy and not a burden. The ascension assures us that, insofar as he has been united with our human nature, the triune God is a God who will not quit until all people are wrapped up in his love. He has made us that kind of people, too. Beside us in these efforts is Jesus, who will not let us quit until all people are wrapped up in his love. The ascension sure is something to celebrate.

Notes

Preface

1. Luther D. Reed, *The Lutheran Liturgy,* rev. ed. (Philadelphia: Fortress Press, 1960), pp. 490-491; George M. Bass, *Lectionary Preaching Workbook: Series III Cycle A* (Lima, Ohio: C.S.S. Publishing Co., 1989), pp. 94-95, 140.

2. See Bass, p. 94, for this observation concerning the role of baptism in Lent.

3. Mark Ellingsen, *Doctrine and Word: Theology in the Pulpit* (Atlanta: John Knox Press, 1983); Mark Ellingsen, *The Evangelical Movement: Growth, Impact, Controversy, Dialog* (Minneapolis: Augsburg Publishing House, 1988); Mark Ellingsen, *The Integrity of Biblical Narrative: Story in Theology and Proclamation* (Minneapolis: Fortress Press, 1990).

Ash Wednesday

1. Martin Luther *Commentary on the Sermon on the Mount* (1532), in *Luther's Works,* eds. Jaroslav Pelikan and Helmut T. Lehmann (55 vols.; St. Louis and Philadelphia: Concordia Publishing House and Fortress Press, 1955-1986), Vol. 21, pp. 132ff.

2. *Ibid.,* p. 135.

Lent 1

1. Eduard Schweizer, *The Good News According to Matthew,* trans. David E. Green (Atlanta: John Knox Press, 1975), pp. 58-60, 65-66. For verification see Josephus, *The Antiquities of the Jews* (93-94), xx. 97.

2. Martin Luther's sermon on Matthew 4:1-11 for Lent 1, his *The Fast and the Temptation of Christ* (1525), 21, in *Sermons of Martin Luther,* ed. John Nicholas Lenker (8 vols.; reprint ed.; Grand Rapids, Mich.: Baker Book House, 1988), Vol. II, p. 144.

3. Martin Luther, *The Large Catechism* (1538), I. 2.

4. Jack Dean Kingsbury, *Matthew As Story* (Philadelphia: Fortress Press, 1986), p. 56.

5. John Calvin, *Institutes of the Christian Religion* (1559), IV/XV.6. Roman Catholic users of this sermon may prefer to employ the following quotation from the Second Vatican Council, *Lumen Gentium* (1964), 7: "Through baptism we are formed in the likeness of Christ . . . with his all-surpassing perfection and activity he fills the whole body with the riches of his glory (cf. Ephesians 1:18-23)."

6. Martin Luther, *Sermons on the Gospel of St. John* (1537-1538), in *Luther's Works,* Vol. 24, p. 83.

Lent 2 (C)
1. The Methodist tradition, following the Anglican/Episcopal heritage, refers to baptism as a "sign" of regeneration. The doctrinal heritage of the Presbyterian Church (USA) and the United Church of Christ also employs this language. See *The Articles of Religion* (1783-1784), 17; *The Thirty-Nine Articles* (1571), XXVII; *The Westminster Confession of Faith* (1646), XXVIII.1. Because the concept of "sign" conveys the idea of the presence of the thing signified, even the least sacramentally oriented members of these traditions must concede that baptism is at least the beginning of regeneration. Yet Wesley himself explicitly affirmed the connection between baptism and regeneration when he wrote in *Short Discourse on Baptism,* II.4, in *A Preservation Against Unsettled Notions in Religion* (1758), that "By water, then, as a means (the water of baptism) we are regenerated or born again." Similarly unambiguous affirmations that regeneration happens in baptism are made by the Lutheran tradition in Martin Luther, *The Large Catechism,* IV.27, and by the Roman Catholic Church in Council of Trent, *Decree Concerning Original Sin,* Fifth Session, 1546, Can. 5; *Baltimore Catechism* (1966), 148.

2. Martin Luther, *Lectures on Galatians* (1535), in *Luther's Works,* Vol. 26, p. 66.

Lent 3 (C), Lent 2 (L), Lent 3 (RC)
1. Martin Luther, *The Freedom of a Christian* (1520), in *Luther's Works,* Vol. 31, p. 351.

Lent 4 (C, RC) Lent 3 (L)
1. For examples of this approach, see Hans W. Frei, *The Eclipse of Biblical Narrative* (New Haven, Ct. and London: Yale University Press, 1974), p. 3; Hans W. Frei, *The Identity of Jesus Christ* (Philadelphia: Fortress Press, 1975), p. xv; George A. Lindbeck, *The Nature of Doctrine* (Philadelphia: Westminster Press, 1984), pp. 118-119; cf. Erich Auerbach, *Mimesis,* trans. Willard Trask (Princeton, N.J.: Princeton University Press, 1953), pp. 14-15.

Lent 4
1. Matthew 27:56 speaks only of the mother of Zebedee's sons, distinguishing her from Mary, the mother of Joseph. (The woman also has some kinship to James, but the Greek does not make the relationship clear.) In the parallel Markan version (15:40-41), there is a reference to Salome, who may be then regarded as the mother of Zebedee's sons. Some have speculated that the mother of these children may have been the sister of Jesus' mother, Mary. In John 19:25ff, Mary's sister is said to stand at her side near the disciple whom Jesus loved (John). Some have speculated that the disciple whom Jesus loved was standing by his mother (Mary's sister). In that case this disciple would have been Jesus' cousin, a consideration which would help account for Jesus' special affection for him and his reasons for entrusting his mother to this disciple (for Mary would have been his aunt).

2. Christopher Lasch, *The Culture of Narcissim* (New York: W.W. Norton & Co., 1979), pp. 116-117, 122.

3. For this view of baptism, as a daily crucifixion of sin for the sake of new life, see Luther, *The Large Catechism,* IV. 65.

Lent 5

1. Martin Luther, *Sermon on the Raising of Lazarus, John 11:1-45, Preached on the Friday after Laetare, March 19, 1518,* in *Luther's Works,* Vol. 51, p. 48. Non-Lutherans may wish to omit this quotation and the preceding sentence.

2. Rudolf Bultmann, *Theology of the New Testament,* trans. Kendrick Grobel (2 vols. in one; New York: Charles Scribner's Sons, 1951, 1955), Vol. I, pp. 44ff; Archibald M. Hunter, *Introducing New Testament Theology* (Philadelphia: The Westminster Press, 1957), pp. 26ff; cf. Hans Conzelmann, *The Theology of St. Luke,* trans., Geoffrey Buswell (New York, Evanston, San Francisco, London: Harper & Row, 1961), pp. 95ff.

Palm Sunday

1. Martin Luther, *Lectures on Romans* (1515-1516), *Luther's Works,* Vol. 25, pp. 382-383.

2. Martin Luther, *Sermon on St. Thomas' Day, Ps. 19:1, December 21, 1516,* in *Luther's Works,* Vol. 51, p. 19.

3. Luther, *Lectures on Romans,* Vol. 25, p. 137.

4. Luther, *Lectures on St. Thomas' Day,* Vol. 51, p. 19.

5. Luther, *Sermons on the Gospel of St. John,* Vol. 24, p. 150.

Maundy Thursday

1. For examples of the agreement among the various denominational traditions concerning the need for repentance and contrition as preparation for the Lord's supper, see *The Invitation to Commune in The United Methodist Church's Liturgy,* in Nolan B. Harmon, *Understanding The United Methodist Church* (rev. ed.; Nashville, Tn.: Abingdon, 1977), p. 130; *The Heidelberg Catechism* (1563), Q. 81; *Baltimore Catechism,* 167; Martin Luther, *Confession and the Lord's Supper* (1524), 20-21, in *Sermons of Martin Luther,* Vol. II, pp. 206-207; Luther, *The Large Catechism,* V. 36-37.

2. R. Alan Culpepper, *Anatomy of the Fourth Gospel: A Study in Literary Design* (Philadelphia: Fortress Press, 1987), p. 118.

3. My sacramental reading of John's comments about the "water" which Jesus bestows as references to baptism is open to some debate among scholars. I am more in line with the thinking of Oscar Cullmann, *Early Christian Worship* (London: SCM Press, 1953), esp. Ch. 2. For a helpful summary of this debate, see James D. G. Dunn, *Unity and Diversity in the New Testament* (Philadelphia: The Westminster Press, 1977), pp. 168-169. The pertinent passages in the debate among scholars about this point are John 2:1-11; 4:7-15; 5:2-9; 7:37-39; 9:7; 13:1-16; 19:34.

4. Even critics of the sacramental reading of John's comments about the "water" which cleanses the faithful will concede that such comments at least refer to the blessing of the new age or to the Holy Spirit who gives these blessings; see Dunn, pp. 169-170; Culpepper, pp. 192-195.

5. See *The First Apology of Justin, The Martyr* (155), 66.

Good Friday

1. See Brevard S. Childs, *The New Testament as Canon: An Introduction* (Philadelphia: Fortress Press, 1985), p. 139.

2. These observations about the modern church's neglect of Christ's sacrificial death (the doctrine of the atonement) have been offered by Jaroslav Pelikan, "Foreward," in Gustaf Aulén, *Christus Victor,* trans. A. G. Hebert (New York: Macmillan, 1969), p. xviii. Also see Langdon Gilkey, *Naming the Whirlwind: The Renewal of God-Language* (Indianapolis and New York: Bobbs-Merrill, 1969), p. 402.

3. For a full and classic description of these viewpoints and their historical development, see Aulén.

4. The view of Christ's death which I articulate is especially inspired by the so-called governmental theory of the atonement, which has been espoused by the leaders of the Holiness movement and the Scandinavian Free Church traditions. See A.M. Hills, *Fundamental Christian Theology,* Vol. II (Pasadena, Cal.: C. J. Kinne, 1931), pp. 42-56, 88-103; H. Orton Wiley, *Christian Theology,* Vol. II (Kansas City, Mo.: Nazarene Publishing House, 1945), pp. 245, 252-259, 273-276; P.P. Waldenstrom, *The Reconciliation,* trans. J.G. Princell (Chicago: John Martenson, 1888), pp. 18, 68, 72-73, 81. For related views in contemporary mainline theology, see Regin Prenter, *Creation and Redemption,* trans. Theodor Jensen (Philadelphia: Fortress Press, 1967). pp. 202-205, 372ff; Wolfhart Pannenberg, *Jesus — God and Man,* trans. Lewis L. Wilkins and Duane A. Priebe (2nd ed.; Philadelphia: The Westminster Press, 1977), pp. 234, 258ff.

5. Childs, p. 137.

The Resurrection Of Our Lord

1. See Rudolf Bultmann, *History of the Synoptic Tradition,* trans. John Marsh (2nd ed.; New York and Evanston, Ill.: Harper & Row, 1968), pp. 287-288; Martin Dibelius, *From Tradition to Gospel,* trans. Bertram Woolf (New York: Charles Scribner's Sons, 1945), pp. 189-190.

Easter 2

1. Martin Luther, *Christ's Resurrection and Its Benefits* (1526), 13, in *Sermons of Martin Luther,* Vol. II, p. 244. Also see Martin Luther, *Commentary on I Corinthians 15* (1532-1533), in *Luther's Works,* Vol. 28, pp. 69-73, 177.

2. Luther, *Lectures on Galatians* (1535), Vol. 26, p. 387. Also see Martin Luther, *The Nature, Fruit, Power and Authority of Faith* (1523/1525), 9, in *Sermons of Martin Luther,* Vol. II, p. 357.

3. Martin Luther, *The Blessed Sacrament of the Holy and True Body of Christ, and the Brotherhoods* (1519), 4-5, 7-11, 14-19, 21-22, in *Luther's Works,* Vol. 35, pp. 50-52, 53-56, 58-62, 65-67.

Easter 3
 1. See Eduard Schweizer, *The Good News According to Luke,* trans. David E. Green (Atlanta: John Knox Press, 1984), pp. 372, 373.
 2. *The Bhagavad-Gita*, trans. Swami Prabhavananda and Christopher Isherwood (New York and Toronto: The New American Library, 1951), p. 75; *[The Buddhist] Digha Nilcaya,*2.64ff, in Wm. Theodore de Barry, ed., *Sources of Indian Tradition,* Vol. I (New York and London: Columbia University Press, 1958), pp. 102-103.

Easter 4
 1. See Ludwig Wittgenstein, *Philosophical Investigations,* 281, trans. G.E.M. Anscombe (3rd ed.; New York: Macmillan, 1958), p. 97; John Dollard and Neal E. Miller, *Personality and Psychotherapy* (New York, Toronto and London: McGraw-Hill, 1950), p. 122.
 2. See Robert N. Bellah, Richard Madsen, William M. Sullivan, Ann Swidler and Steven M. Tipton, *Habits of the Heart* (New York: Harper & Row, 1986), esp. pp. 75-76, 82-83.
 3. Martin Luther, *Christ's Office and Kingdom* (1523), 8, in *Sermons of Martin Luther,* Vol. III, p. 21.
 4. Bellah et al, esp. pp. 48, 50, 139-141.
 5. Martin Luther, *Christ's Person, Office and Government* (1543), 45, in *Sermons of Martin Luther,* Vol. III, p. 62.

Easter 5
 1. Bellah et al, esp. pp. 226, 232-233.
 2. Luther, *Sermons on the Gospel of St. John,* Vol. 24, p. 64.

Easter 6
 1. Luther, *The Freedom of a Christian,* Vol. 31, p. 351. Lutheran pastors may wish to employ the full quotation. It appears on p. 45 of this volume.
 2. Calvin, *Institutes of the Christian Religion,* IV/VII.2. cf. Luther, *Sermons on the Gospel of St. John,* Vol. 24, p. 141.
 3. Luther, *Sermons on the Gospel of St. John,* Vol. 24, pp. 114-115.
 4. Also see *Ibid.*, p. 158.
 5. *Ibid.*, p. 146.

Easter 7
 1. Augustine, *On the Trinity,* 5.5.6.
 2. *Ibid.*, 6.5.7. Also see Schweizer, *The Good News According to Matthew,* p. 533.

3. The model of unity which I espouse here, "unity in reconciled diversity," is discussed in some detail by Gunther Gassmann and Harding Meyer, *The Unity of the Church: Requirements and Structure* in *LWF Report,* 15 (June 1983).

4. Carl F.H. Henry, *God, Revelation and Authority,* Vol. V (Waco, Texas: Word Books, 1982), p. 213.

5. Martin Luther, *The Resurrection of Christ* (1538), 14, in *Sermons of Martin Luther,* Vol. II, pp. 254-255.

Ascension Day/Ascension Sunday (C, L)

1. See Martin Luther, *Christ's Commission to His Disciples to Preach the Gospel: Christ's Ascension* (1523), 24, in *Sermons of Martin Luther,* Vol. III, p. 190.

Ascension Day/Ascension Sunday (RC)

1. See Schweizer, *The Good News According to Matthew,* p. 528.

2. For a discussion of the hypothesis that the transfiguration account was originally a resurrection story, see Bultmann, *History of the Synoptic Tradition,* pp. 259-260.

3. Luther, *Christ's Commission to His Disciples to Preach the Gospel: Christ's Ascension (1523), 24,* in *Sermons of Martin Luther,* Vol. III, p. 192.

4. Augustine, *On the Trinity,* 6.5.7.